History of Montague County

Fannie "Mrs. W.R. Potter"] [Potter

Nabu Public Domain Reprints:

You are holding a reproduction of an original work published before 1923 that is in the public domain in the United States of America, and possibly other countries. You may freely copy and distribute this work as no entity (individual or corporate) has a copyright on the body of the work. This book may contain prior copyright references, and library stamps (as most of these works were scanned from library copies). These have been scanned and retained as part of the historical artifact.

This book may have occasional imperfections such as missing or blurred pages, poor pictures, errant marks, etc. that were either part of the original artifact, or were introduced by the scanning process. We believe this work is culturally important, and despite the imperfections, have elected to bring it back into print as part of our continuing commitment to the preservation of printed works worldwide. We appreciate your understanding of the imperfections in the preservation process, and hope you enjoy this valuable book.

Potter, Fannie (Bellows) "Mrs. W.R. Potter"

COUNTY SERIES READER

HISTORY *of* MONTAGUE COUNTY

ERA 1—*Immigration*
ERA 2—*Organization*
ERA 3—*Progress*

E. L. STECK　　AUSTIN

"The American Republic is not leagues and furlongs; it is not wealth; it is not power. It is embodied liberty, regulated by law; it is liberty resting upon organized institutions, through which society and civilization may blossom into their fullest and fairest flower."

EXPLANATION.

It was the first purpose of the author of this book to write a history that would only be read in the homes of the county; but, after much deliberation and consultation with those best fitted to know, it was decided to condense the work and put it in a form that could be studied as a supplementary reader in the public schools of this county.

Believing that such a study would tend to cultivate that patriotism which is the heritage of every American citizen, and cause our youths to look with a greater degree of reverence upon the early settlers of this county, the writer makes this explanation for the benefit of those who have so kindly given the data which this book contains, that they may know why some of the smaller details are left out. The sketches of Indian depredations necessarily had to be condensed for school purposes. The author also wishes to express a sincere appreciation to the following friends who have assisted greatly in the compiling of this history: Mr. Bud Morris, Mr. Cash McDonald, Mr. C. Moore, Mr. C. Grant, Mr. Joe Box, Mr. Bob Savage, Mr. Levi Perryman, Mr. W. R. Bellows, Mr. S. G. Dowell, Mrs. Charlie Moore, Mrs. Charlie Grant, Mrs. Levi Blankenship, Mrs. Nettie Bellows, Mrs. Bob Savage, Mrs. Chesley Marlett.

PREFACE:

This book, partially, owes its origin to the encouragement of friends, who, long ago, urged me to attempt a work which would serve to illustrate and perpetuate the epoch-making periods of the history of Montague County. I have never wished more earnestly than now that these pages were possessed of a merit which might outlive my time, so at least these lines might remain as a record of the excellence of the people whom I loved and among whom it is my pleasure to live.

The genuine hardihood and true nobility of the pioneers of our county have never been fully appreciated. Their deeds of heroism and courage equalled those enacted by their ancestors in the early days of the "Colonies." There were dangers untold, dreadful days and nights of anxiety; Indian battles were fought, fierce and long; many a father, many a brother, sleeps where he fell, the forgotten, silent hero of civilization's advance.

Naturally, too, the interests of these pioneer people became interwoven with each other, and, as will be seen, when Indian dangers lurked, and the mutterings of war were heard throughout the land, they were drawn still closer together, and the citizens became as brothers, with the same feelings stirring their hearts.

I would not give the men the praise alone, for

many a covered wagon, as it rolled away from home and loved ones bore many a tearful, heartsore daughter as she bade farewell to father and mother to follow the fortunes of her husband, who, answering the call of the wild, determined to make for themselves a home in the beautiful west. Dangers lurked on every hand, but they were brave; privations awaited them, but they were enduring. Hope deferred, which maketh the heart sick, was theirs, but God gave them patience. What a heritage of progress, power and strength they have given us.

In attempting this work I have endeavored to study the times and characters diligently. In these pages I have tried to represent the history as it was and is. As a people we are prone to go beyond the limits of home for talent, progress and beauty of scenery, but I venture to hope the reader will obtain from these pages a better opinion of the importance of the county in which we live. More especially do I hope to perpetuate the memory of those "makers of history," the noble pioneer men and women who endured privations and hardships, battlings with the Indians, and the internal strifes incident to the civil war, that the foundation for a successful and progressive citizenship might be made. It is to these men and women this book is most respectfully dedicated by the author.

MRS. W. R. POTTER.

Bowie, Texas.

CONTENTS.

	PAGE
Texas	1
Early History of Austin	5
Indians—Some of their characteristics	8
Sad Fate of Daniel Wainscot and Jack Kilgore	13
Example of Indian Cruelties to Animals	19
Death of Spencer Moore and His Son, Ira	21
Attack on Jim Box and His Family	24
An Exciting Chase	27
The Fate of One Indian	28
Death of Two Young Boys	29
Indians Slay Nathan Long	31
Capture of the McElroy Children	38
Indians Charge on Mr. Jackson's Home	40
Death of Lieutenant Van Roberts	42
Another Indian Raid	47
Indian Raid Near Spanish Fort	51
Capture of Dick Freeman and John Bailey	53
The Lost Soldier	59
Among Other Indian Cruelties	63
An Indian Attack	65
Queen's Peak Incident	66
Old Tip's Dislike for the Indians	68
Indians Disturb Preaching Service	71
An Indian Skirmish	75
A Pioneer Woman's Experience With the Indians	75
Death of Andy Powers	77

CONTENTS.

	PAGE
Indian Cunning	78
Brother and Sister Defend Their Mother's Home	80
Fate of the Keenan and Paschal Families	87
Easter Sunday, 1871	93
Story of Beale and Maxey Families	94
Charging Victoria Peak, summer of 1870	98
Indian Masquerades as Woman	99
Indians Attack Lee Home	101
Satanta	102
The Indian Crossing	106
The Last Indian Raid in Montague County	107
Jim Ned Look Out	114
Brushy Mound	115
The Home of My Early Days	118
The Home Life of the Pioneer	119
To the Boys and Girls	128
I'll Do What I Can	130
Ode to Montague County	131
Montague County	133
Texas Rangers	146
The Southland	149
The United Daughters of the Confederacy	150
The Old Coat of Gray	157
United Confederate Veterans	159
Progressive Montague County	163
Patriotism	184

TEXAS.

Blessed are all free people,
  Too strong to be dispossessed,
But blessed are those among nations,
  Who dare to be strong for the rest."

One bright spring morning Tom was strolling about the capitol grounds in Austin. Now, Tom was not of a very artistic temperament, but the scene was so beautiful that even he could not help but admire it. All nature was out in holiday attire. The air was fragrant with dewy blossoms. The Texas blue bonnets were waving a cordial welcome, and over all shone the blue of a Texas sky. I wish, pupils, that you would study with your teacher the wonderful colorings in our Texas sky. It would soon have a peculiar charm for you. Sometimes it grows angry, and the mutterings of thunder is heard, and it darts vivid tongues of lightning in your path. Again it is as peaceful as a New England Sabbath—with the most exquisite colorings of blue and yellow and gold, with softened tints of gray. At other times wearing a soft pink, like the blush on a Texas maiden's cheek.

"The sky is a drinking cup,
  That was overturned of old,
And it pours in the eyes of men
  Its wine of airy gold;
We drink that wine all day,
  Till the last drop is drained up,
And are lighted to our bed
  By the jewels in the cup."

As Tom strolled about, his footsteps led him to a handsome granite monument. Let me see to whom this monument is erected. As he read the historic inscription engraved upon it, he saw that this was the silent tribute of honor erected to the memory of those noble Texas heroes who loyally gave their lives for the cause they loved so well; that cause so dear to every American heart, Liberty. Engraved upon this monument were these sad but significant words, "Thermopylae had her messenger of defeat, the Alamo had none."

Now, Tom had been a diligent student of Texas history, just as you will be later on, and quite naturally his thoughts turned to that scene in the old mission building. In his imagination he could see the immortal Travis as he gathered his little band of brave men about him, and how gallantly they perished for Texas, and how the cruel Santa Anna had their bodies burned. Mrs. Pennybacker, in her History of Texas, says: "As the Sabbath sun sank slowly in the west, the smoke from that funeral pyre of heroes ascended to heaven. From that sacred fire sprang the flames that lighted all Texas, that consumed many Mexican lives, and caused even the Napoleon of the West to bow low his haughty head." One of the last official acts of President Tyler was to sign a bill providing for the annexation of Texas to the Union, making it a law. On February 19th, 1846, Texas became subject to the laws of the United States, after the people had voted almost unanimously in favor of it. Never did the United States of America receive a fairer daughter. With her trees, her streams, her flower decked prairies, she brought with her men of brain and brawn; women of faith and courage; she brought with her an empire territory, exceeding in extent most of the governments of the world. Texas brought the United States an area of 265,780 square miles, or 170,926,080 acres. Its greatest extent from north to south is 760 miles, and 740 miles from east to west.

The public school system of Texas ranks well with that of other States, although our public educators are not entirely satisfied with the present system, but are constantly reaching out along more progressive lines. Texas comprises a variety of soil and climate, and its productions are of equal variety. Texas ranks first among the States in many lines of production and industry. She is first in area, railway mileage, cotton, cattle, mules, goats, honey, pecans, turkeys, and watermelons. She also ranks well in the raising of grain, hogs and poultry.

Swiftly flowing streams, along whose banks the "children of the forest" were wont to roam in the long ago, have given place to thriving towns and progressive cities. The noisy brook goes hurrying by as it babbles to us of Texas, her glorious past, her gracious present, and her magnificent future.

From East Texas, where it has been said "the pine trees grow so tall they tickle the feet of the angels," to West Texas, where the green pastures provide for the cattle on a thousand hills; from North Texas on to where the Gulf of Mexico laves her southern shores, Texas is teeming with the splendid gifts which nature has bestowed upon her, and the smoke curls peacefully from thousands of happy homes. See the great tide of immigration that is constantly flowing across her borders. From the east, from the west, and from far to the north of us they come. All the States contributing to this great commonwealth of ours.

On the morning mentioned in the beginning Tom's thoughts dwelt again on the monument upon which their names stood out in bold relief. He reviewed the path of progress made possible by these heroic men, and he said aloud: "Ah! Bonham, Travis, Crockett, Bowie, you builded far better than you knew." And now, pupils, are you not glad that our own county of Montague forms a part of this great

State, with its vast resources, and its wonderful history?

In the following chapters you must pay especial attention to the part your county plays in Texas—the Lone Star State.

EARLY HISTORY OF AUSTIN.

It is fitting that every boy and girl in our county should be familiar with the location of our State capital. It is the capital for Montague county, just as it is for the other counties which go to make up the great State of Texas. Let us see what we can learn that will be of interest to us. First, we find that six years before Texas was made a part of the United States the founders of the "Republic of Texas," of which you will learn more when you take up the study of State history, appointed a commission to select a place for a permanent seat of government. This city they named Austin, in honor of the founder of Texas. It is situated near the center of the State, on the Colorado River, in Travis County. It is here that our magnificent granite capitol building stands. This building is located near the center of the city, and from its upper stories a commanding view of the country is to be had. From east to west this building is 600 feet long; from north to south, 287 feet deep, and the height of the apex of the dome is 313 feet, being six feet higher than our national capitol at Washington, D. C. The exterior walls are built of Texas red granite, brought from the quarries of Burnet County. This granite is pronounced by experts to be as fine as any in the world. Wherever it was possible, Texas material has been used in the building, and nearly all the material is native growth. There are 258 rooms, 900 windows and 500 doors. The wainscoting is made of oak, ash, pine, cedar, cherry, mahogany and walnut—the aggregate length of which is said to be about seven miles. The building covers three acres of ground, and has about eighteen acres of floor space. A Chicago syndicate erected this capitol building for a consideration of three million acres of Texas land. The building was begun in 1882 and completed in 1888. So, you see, they were six years building this great capitol, of which Texas people are justly proud. And why not take a pride in it? With the exception of the capitol building at Washington it is the largest building in the United States, and the seventh largest building in the world. Do not forget this fact. It may be your privilege to visit Austin some time and go through this great structure. When you go, do not fail to go over the beautiful grounds. You will find miles of cement and gravel walks, leading in all directions; you will see beautiful fountains, artificial lakes and pools, sparkling in the sunshine, and in which the gold fish are swimming about, while beautiful plants of gorgeous hue are blooming on every side.

Be sure you visit the "Capitol Green House." This beautiful addition to the capitol grounds was erected under the supervision of a former Montague County citizen, Mr. W. C. Day, while he was Superintendent of Public Buildings and Grounds during the Campbell administration. You will recognize this green house by a single large gold star over the entrance. The flowers grown here are for use in the Governor's mansion, just across the way, and are of many and rare varieties.

On the left of the broad walk leading to the main entrance to the capitol you will see the Terry Rangers' and the Firemen's monuments, and on the right side two monuments dear to every Texan's heart, one erected to the Confederacy, the other to the heroes of the Alamo.

The two main departments of this great capitol building are the Senate chamber and the House of Representatives. The Daughters of the Confederacy have a room set apart for their especial use. In this room many war relics are preserved that serve to perpetuate the history of our Southland. There are numerous other offices in the capitol building occupied by the various State officers. There is also a handsomely furnished reception room, set apart for the Governor's use.

Across the street from the capitol building is the

Governor's mansion, a fine old colonial building that has been the home for so many Texas Governors and their families.

INDIANS—SOME OF THEIR CHARACTERISTICS

"Alas! the poor Indian,
With untutored mind,
Finds God in the clouds,
And again in the wind."

But little is known of the real origin of the North American Indian. Many historians, with as many different theories, have undertaken to account for the presence of the Indians in the New World, but to this good hour the problem remains practically unsolved. All writers agree, however, that they are among the oldest races of mankind. After much study, all writers have much the same things to say about the Indian.

As to pursuits, they rarely cared to cultivate the soil, but were truly men of the chase. To hunt was the Indian's favorite pastime. They were never more contented than in a country of forests, hills and streams, where they could hunt the bear, deer and other wild game. In disposition the Indian is silent and unsocial, often answering the politest question with a grunt or nod. With all that has been done for the Indian toward their civilization, by church and school, their nature remains much the same. The Indian woman, or squaw, as she was generally called, was nothing more than a slave for her warrior husband.

As to religion, the Indians were a superstitious race. They believed in a Great Spirit; they believed He ruled the elements, rewarded the faithful and punished the wicked. They built no churches, such as we have; the medicine man was looked upon with much awe and respect, and they listened to his sayings. The happy hunting ground of his imagination was his only idea of a home in the great beyond. Often the trappings of a warrior were buried with him, that he might be prepared for a continuation of the sports and pastimes enjoyed here.

The Indian had a great love for war. Revenge was his watchword. To forgive, to show any sign of sympathy or regret was considered a weakness. They were cunning and treacherous. To meet a foe in the open was not to their liking. They delighted to lie in wait and spring upon him unawares. Their especial pleasure was to torture their captives, and it was in this fiendish pastime that the real savage nature shone without reserve. His home was a wigwam. His clothing, for the most part, consisted of a blanket thrown over his shoulders, sometimes bound about him, and at other times worn as a loosely flowing robe. They sometimes wore hats to deceive the settlers into thinking they were white men. He delighted to adorn himself with beaded ornaments, to paint his face in bright colors, and, more than all, he prized the scalp of the white man as an especial adornment. Dressed in this manner, and with unearthly yells, did he like to descend upon an unsuspecting settler and his family to kill and scalp them, take some captive and lay waste their home, kill their cattle and steal their horses.

The great warfare between the white man and the Indian (as we all know) began when the white man determined to take from the Indian his home. Inch by inch they contested every foot of the land of their fathers. Step by step, through stealth and strife, through war and bloodshed, they have been driven on by the progress due to civilization, until now, indolent and indifferent, subdued and satisfied, it is difficult to think of them as having been the warlike tribes that history describes. An early writer of the history of Northwest Texas tells us "that it is doubtful if any State has suffered more severely at the hands of the Indians than has Texas. From its earliest days they were a constant menace to all efforts at civilization and permanent habitation. The name Apache and Comanche have become synonymous for ferocity and bloodthirstiness and the worst traits of savagery. And for years the tribes of that race harassed the frontier and carried their warfare into the heart of the settlements."

The history of Indian warfare and outrage in Texas would fill volumes. During the period of which this is written, the sole ambition of the Indians who raided Montague County was to steal horses and exterminate the whites. The settlers noticed certain peculiarities belonging to the Indians. If they recovered a stolen horse, and it had its ears split, they knew the Comanches had stolen it. If it had one ear split and the other ear cropped, they knew the Kiowas had stolen it. They learned to look for Indian raids on moonlight nights. We, of today, look forward to our beautiful moonlight nights with pleasure; it is then we delight to have our moonlight socials, our protracted meetings, and to visit our friends. Not so in early days. These were nights of anxiety and dread to the settler. They observed that the fiercest dog would not molest an Indian, nor would it even bark if a large band of Indians were to surround his master's house at night. The exact cause of this is unknown—some attributed it to fear, others thought it was due to some charm the Indian cast over the dog. The Indian was also master of the art of handling horses. He could take a horse that a white man considered tired and worn out from a long day's ride and had exhausted all efforts to make him travel faster. The Indian could mount the same horse and by some unknown means cause him to travel equal to a fresh horse. The Indian had many forms of amusement—among them the war dance. In conducting this dance sometimes the warriors danced alone, but frequently the women were permitted to join in the dance, too. They circled around and around, meanwhile chanting the weird, monotonous songs of their tribes. These dances have been the means of attracting large crowds to many of the western towns where on such occasions as barbecues, county fairs, etc., the Indians are persuaded to attend and give their dance for the amusement of the onlookers. They had other amusements, such as wrestling, running, leaping, shooting at a mark, racing in canoes and many other games. They were much given to the gambling spirit, and in a moment of excitement would sometimes wager all they possessed. They love tobacco, and it has been said that no race has succumbed so quickly to the liquor habit. It was with these wild untutored people, who gave no mercy nor asked any, that the early settlers of Montague and adjoining counties had to battle for the homes of peace and plenty we now enjoy.

In the following pages will be given, in condensed form, a list of "Indian Depredations" and their dates—not all the county suffered, but enough for the boys and girls of today to know and to appreciate the dangers the pioneers endured:

SAD FATE OF DANIEL WAINSCOT AND JACK KILGORE, AND THRILLING EXPERIENCE OF MRS. BOB WAINSCOT.

In 1858 John Willingham and Bob Wainscot built for themselves a substantial log cabin in what was then called Buchanan Valley, but is now known as the Frank Biggers place, on Denton Creek, it being the custom in those days for two or more families to live together for protection from the Indians. This portion of Montague County offered many inducements for the industrious man, and as they builded their home and surveyed the fertile little valley, future hopes ran high. On September 4 their families arrived. The following day being Sunday they went to the home of Daniel Wainscot. There they found a large company, about thirty in number, assembled to spend the day. We can imagine them enjoying the hospitality of this good pioneer home. The women are busy preparing dinner, as they discuss their everyday home lives. Occasionally a shadow of fear crosses their faces, and an unexpected noise causes them to turn pale, for danger may be lurking near. Their anxious looks linger longest on their little ones, and very tenderly they smooth the curly heads and kiss the rosy cheeks, and a mist comes before their eyes as they ever remember that the dreaded Indian foe has no mercy on babies. But the ringing laughter of the children at play in the sunshine dispels their momentary fear, and they take up the thread of conversation anew. The men in the front yard talked of everyday affairs, and gave an occasional word of warning to the newcomers about the Indians.

The day being clear and sunshiny, the entire company decided to go over to the new Willingham and Wainscot place, as they expressed it, just to pass the time. The following were in the number: Cash McDonald and family, Daniel Wainscot and family, Bob Wainscot and family, John Willingham and family, Fine McFarland, Ike Wainscot, Jack Kilgore and family.

Cash McDonald drove his wagon, with a yoke of steers hitched to it, and a number of the women and children rode with him, the others walking leisurely along by its side, as steers do not travel fast. Bob Wainscot and Jack Kilgore were a little in advance of the wagon. When they reached a point of timber, about a quarter of a mile from the new house, without a word of warning seven Indians sprang out from the woods upon them, uttering unearthly yells as they came. Seeing their approach to the house was cut off by the Indians the men turned to run back to the wagon. Just after they reached it both men were slain by the Indians. By this time the women and children had scattered like frightened birds, some going in one direction and some in another. Contrary to their custom, the Indians did not take time to scalp their victims, but turned their attention to the rest of the party. All the members of the company managed to reach the home of John Wainscot in safety, with the exception of Cash McDonald and Mrs. Bob Wainscot. Mr. McDonald held in his arms his two-year-old daughter, Mary (now Mrs. Andy Jackson of Bowie). He was shot in the arm with an arrow, but fortunately little Mary was unhurt. Notwithstanding this, he walked twelve miles, shunning the road, for fear of Indians, still carrying the child in his arms, reaching Bill Freeman's house in the night. They pulled the arrow from his arm, which had remained there all of these hours, and was very painful. Mrs. Bob Wainscot also had a thrilling experience. In the confusion following the attack by the Indians she became separated from her husband. Looking back, she saw an Indian shoot her husband, who fell with their four-year-old daughter in his arms. She supposed both were killed, but the Indians passed on and they made their way to safety. She proceeded on her way, running with her six-weeks-old baby in her arms. (Now Mrs. Huse Wainscot of Denver.) She came upon Mr. Cash McDonald, who, as has already been told, had his little daughter with him. The child was sick, and crying aloud for her mother. They could not quiet her by any means, so Mr. McDonald said, "If Mary continues to cry this way she may attract the Indians, and they will come and kill us all. It is hard for you to start out through the woods alone, but it may be the means of saving your life and that of your baby." It was a fearful moment, but the half distracted woman decided to take his advice and started through the woods alone. Having just come into the neighborhood the day before she was wholly unacquainted with the country. Her one thought was to travel in the direction of the old home she had left. On and on the terror stricken woman went. She traveled all the afternoon and that night over stones and hollows, through briars and thickets; the next day found her between Bradin's Bluff and Clear Creek, having traveled in her wanderings about thirty miles. In all this time she had eaten but two wild plums. About 12 o'clock that day, hungry and almost exhausted, she paused to rest for a short time near a hollow. In the beginning of her flight she had lost her sunbonnet. Her hair had become loosened and fell about her face in such a manner that her features could not be discerned without close scrutiny. A band of white men, who had heard of the raid and started out to aid in the capture of the Indians, came upon Mrs. Wainscot quite suddenly. Seeing her long black hair falling in Indian fashion about her face they mistook her for an Indian squaw and paused an instant before approaching, not knowing what might await them. She caught a glimpse of the men, and believing them to be Indians, she ran with her baby clasped to her breast. She hid in a washed out place in the hillside. The men found her there, and she was overjoyed to learn they were white men. She poured out her story to them between sobs. One of the men took her behind him on his horse, while another carried the baby in his arms. They took her to the home of Mr. John Wainscot, where to her great joy she found her husband and little daughter.

The remains of the two men who were slain by the Indians were removed to the home of Anderson White. As his house was the largest in the neighborhood the entire settlement was invited to come there and stay until after the funerals of Jack Kilgore and Daniel Wainscot, which they accepted. The next morning they were both buried in the same grave, in what is now known as Frank Bigger's field. They had to be wrapped in blankets as there were no coffins nearer than Gainesville, or Decatur, many miles away, and with the way beset by perils on every side. They laid them to rest 'neath two widespreading trees, and the summer sun shines and the winter snows fall softly upon the graves of two of the martyrs to the civilization we now enjoy.

This was one of the first massacres by the Indians to occur in Montague County that we have record of. After the Indians left the scene of the killing of the two men just recounted they came up on Mr. Bud

Morris of Montague, who was out hunting cows. He was riding a fine horse. He outran the Indians and escaped without injury. This same band of Indians went on to Hardy, about four miles from Forestburg, and stole forty head of horses from Doctor Polly. Dr. Polly was one of the pioneer physicians of Montague County. He was also the first county judge of Montague County. He is described as being a natural leader and a useful citizen. The country was to thinly settled at this time that his judicial duties in no way interfered with his practice of medicine.

After the killing of Jack Kilgore and Daniel Wainscot the people of the settlement stayed in families for protection from the Indians. Many of them packed up their belongings and moved near Gainesville to be out of reach of the Indians. They came back the following November to the same homes. Nothing had been molested, but things were just as they had left them. The woods at this time were full of wolves, some bear, deer, wild cats and panther. Wild turkey was plentiful, and it has been said that nothing was more appetizing than slices from the breast of a turkey (they never thought of eating any other portion of it), broiled or fried a delicate golden brown, with rich brown gravy; a hoe cake of corn bread and a cup of steaming hot coffee. There was also an abundance of wild duck, geese and prairie chicken, which was much relished.

So the settlers had no scarcity of meat, so far as wild game was concerned.

EXAMPLE OF INDIAN CRUELTY TO ANIMALS.

On the tenth of May, 1858, there moved into the community of Victoria Peak, now known as "Queen's Peak," Uncle Johnnie Roe and a man named Cryner. They had not had time to build houses, so were camped in tents and covered wagons. They turned their horses out to graze that night. Mr. Cryner had a lariat rope on his horse, and Mr. Roe had iron hobbles on two mares and colts. In the night the Indians came and stole Mr. Cryner's horse. Not knowing how to take the iron hobbles off the other horses, and not wishing to leave them for the benefit of the white men, they cut their legs off, taking the iron hobbles with them. They did not molest the campers.

In a few days followed the killing by John Bradin. A party of men hearing how the Indians had mutilated Mr. Roe's horses, started to search for them. There were five white men in the party, among them John Bradin. When about four miles northwest of where Montague now stands, at a place called "Barrel Springs," they came up on two Indians with a bunch of stolen horses. In the encounter which followed, John Bradin killed one of the Indians. They scalped him and the other Indian ran away, leaving the stolen horses. Mr. Bradin had an old British yagur (now called musket), with which he slew the Indian. He himself was killed after the war.

THE KILLING OF LITTLE HENRY DAVIS.

In February, 1859, Bill Davis, who lived in Grayson County, came to this county to visit at the home of his stepfather, Anderson White, who lived on Denton Creek. He brought with him his little son, Henry. They had previously known Mrs. McFarland and her children, and as they passed the house on their way to Mr. White's, Henry begged to be allowed to stop and play with the McFarland children. His father consented to this, but told him to go to Bill Taylor's about 2 o'clock to feed and water some mules he had left there. When the hour came Henry obediently started on his way. When about half way there the little fellow came up on a band of Indians. The boy, like any other child under like circumstances, started to run. The Indians gave chase, and ran him over a steep bank into a hole of water. He made his way to the opposite bank. They followed, killed and scalped him. On this same morning a man named Truelove had gone with a band of men to help trail a band of Indians. In the afternoon he separated from the party and started for his home in the Perryman settlement. Without warning he suddenly came upon this band of Indians killing little Henry Davis. He ran with all his might, crying loudly for help. As he neared the McFarland home, Mrs. McFarland ran out with a gun to assist him. Together they succeeded in frightening away the Indians that had followed him. He then told of the boy the Indians were killing as he came up. She at once thought it was Henry Davis. A searching party went to see and found it to be only too true. When they found him his small boyish face was turned toward the setting sun, his mutilated body bearing evidence of another innocent little life being sacrificed to gratify Indian cruelty. He was buried on the Wiley B. Savage place, on Denton Creek, seven miles south of Montague.

DEATH OF SPENCER MOORE AND HIS SON, IRA, AT THE HANDS OF A BAND OF INDIANS.

In a lonely cabin, near Pittman Hollow, in February, 1863, lived Spencer Moore, his wife and large family of children. Life, to this good pioneer man was a stern reality.

It had been a problem with him as to how he would provide for so large a family in this frontier country.

Only one son, Ira, was large enough to be of any assistance to his father in the labor of breadwinning for the family. They had succeeded in getting some rails to maul from Lewis Davis of that neighborhood. On the day of which I am about to tell you, Mr. Moore and his son were busy with their work. As they worked they talked cheerily together, for that evening Mr. Davis was going to pay them for their entire work, and that meant money enough to buy plenty of corn for bread for the remainder of the year. How the burden rolled away as the father realized that by his labor he would be enabled to provide for his dependent family in this simple though necessary way. The noise of mauling the rails could be heard quite a distance through the woods. About 2 o'clock in the afternoon one of the neighbors, Mr. Cash McDonald, noticed that the sound had ceased. The continued silence alarmed him, for in "Indian times" everything of this kind was taken notice of. The silence finally became oppressive, for the ringing blows of the rail makers were not heard again. Thoroughly aroused Mr. McDonald and others went to the field to find their fears to be only too true. Spencer Moore and his son had both been killed and scalped by the Indians. They supposed the boy had tried to fight with his axe and perhaps wounded some of the Indians from the quantity of blood scattered about.

John Wainscot brought a wagon and took the bodies to his house, where they remained until burial. Ike Wainscot, just a boy, but with all the manliness and kindly spirit which characterized the older pioneers, insisted that Ira be buried in his Sunday shirt. And Sunday shirts were hard to get in those days. Father and son were buried in the Denver graveyard. The good people of the community provided for the widow and helpless children. They gave her provisions enough to last a long time and cared for her until she moved to Denton County, where she was in no danger from the Indians.

It transpired that the Indians who did the killing had been raiding through Jack County, stealing horses from the wheat fields. A crowd of men determined to surprise them, and secreted themselves in a near by wheat field. It was a bright moonlight night and the Indians could be plainly seen by the waiting men as they rode up bent on stealing their horses. They opened fire on the Indians, wounding one and possibly more, but they were carried away by their companions, who, seeing their disadvantage, turned and fled with the white men in pursuit. They lost their trail and the Indians crossed over into Montague County, and on their way stopped long enough to murder Spencer Moore and his son, Ira.

ATTACK ON JIM BOX AND FAMILY BY THE INDIANS.

Mr. Jim Box, together with his family, lived in Montague County, at the "Head of Elm," where the town of St. Jo now stands. In August, 1866, he was returning home from a visit in East Texas, accompanied by his family, when they were attacked by a band of Indians.

It was the custom in those days for men, before starting on a journey, to get up on some high place and look out over the surrounding country to discover if Indians were near. On this occasion Charlie Grant, Bill Grant, John Loving and Zeke Huffman rode up on what was known as Wheeler's Mound, about a quarter of a mile from the road, to see if the coast was clear. To their horror they saw a band of Indians surrounding the wagon in which were Mr. Box and his family. Mrs. Box, who held her baby in her arms, managed to get out of the wagon and, followed by her three daughters, started to run. They were so badly frightened they scarcely realized what they were doing. While the Indians were slaying Mr. Box they ran first from the wagon, then back again two or three times. Resistance was useless, so they were captured and carried off by the Indians. The men who witnessed the killing were unable to render any assistance, as they were unarmed and far outnumbered by the Indians. To attract their attention meant certain death to them. They went to the home of Charlie Grant's father for arms and reinforcements. They returned to the scene of the killing that night to search for the body of Jim Box, accompanied by a man named Cherry and a one-armed negro called Old Jack Loring. Mr. Box had purchased a large quantity of leather, which he had with him. They found the leather, together with the other contents of the wagon, scattered over the prairie. It was a dark misty night, making it hard to distinguish objects. The Indians had torn open a large feather bed and scattered the feathers everywhere. They clung to the wet broom weeds, and were scattered over Mr. Box's fallen body. The men rode around the wagon several times before they found him. He had been scalped. They did not remove the body until the next day, but rode the rest of the night getting up a posse to follow the Indians. Jim Coursey and Captain Brunson and others followed them and found the dead body of Mrs. Box's little baby. Mrs. Box and her three daughters were held as captives on the Canadian River for some time. Friends intervened in their behalf and they were finally bought back by the government and returned to their home in Montague County. They were accompanied home by Lieutenant Harmon and his company of Fort Sill. Mrs. Box, who afterwards became the wife of Captain Brunson, told the following story of their thrilling experience with the Indians:

After killing her husband they tied her on a wild horse and speared him to make him plunge. The plunging of the horse caused her to drop her baby. The Indians picked the poor little thing up and killed it before her eyes, and took the party on across Red River. There were nineteen Indians in the band. They refused to give Mrs. Box water, although she was so thirsty her tongue was swollen from her mouth. One of her daughters took off her slipper and filled it with water as they crossed a stream. She gave it to her mother. Her mother managed to drink it before the Indians could dash it from her lips. They took a leather quirt and beat the daughter almost to death for this act of kindness to her heartbroken mother. The Indians separated the family, putting them in different camps. The little girl, eight years old, would cry and run after the other members of the family when she would see them. The Indians held her feet to the fire until they were blistered, so she could not follow her mother and sisters. It is hard to realize that such barbarous acts ever took place in this county, but all the cruelties the early settlers suffered at the hands of the Indians will never be known.

EXCITING CHASE AND FIGHT WITH INDIANS.

About this time there were numerous small depredations by the Indians and the settlers were in constant dread of their coming. On a certain morning in September, 1866, another band of Indians came into Montague County. They passed the fort at the head of Elm and exchanged shots with the men stationed there.

They went east about four miles and killed a man named Jim Harris. The Indians then passed on in the direction of Gainesville, killing Andy Powers, a citizen of Montague County. Near there this band was joined by another band of Indians.

They passed up the ridge between Clear Creek and Elm Creek, back into Montague County, with about five hundred stolen horses. Charlie Grant, with a posse of forty men, followed them into Clay County and on to the Big Wichita River. The night before a band of men had started from Red River Station in pursuit of this same party of Indians. They had crossed the Big Wichita River and had a battle with the Indians, there being about twenty-five white men against more than a hundred Indians. The white men, when they struck the Indian trail, the day before, knowing that Charlie Grant and his men were coming behind, stuck a stick in the ground, in a place where they would be sure to find it, and tied a note on it bearing these words: "Come on, boys; they have passed this way." The determined men pressed on, but were soon confronted by different orders. They found this message tacked on a tree on the banks of the Big Wichita River: "Turn back, boys; they have given us a warm reception."

After their battle with the Indians, the whites, finding themselves to be far outnumbered by the enemy, decided to retreat. When the last party of white men came to the place where the orders were tacked on the tree, they followed the advice and returned to their homes.

THE FATE OF ONE INDIAN.

After the killing of Tom Fitzpatrick and his wife, and the capture of their two little daughters by the Indians, the father of Tom Fitzpatrick continued to live at the old home place alone. He was very deaf. One night a band of Indians surrounded the house. They fired quite a number of shots into the house, as was discovered next day, before they succeeded in arousing the old man, who was sound asleep. When he awoke and finally decided that the Indians were attacking the house he began firing at them. This frightened the Indians and they turned to run. In their path was an old abandoned well, about forty yards from the house. One of the Indians rode into the well. His horse plunging head foremost into the well, carried his unfortunate rider with him. Some of the neighbors came next day and succeeded in getting the Indian out. The fall had killed him. The horse was left in the well. This farm is north of Forrestburg two miles and is now known as the Ben Steadham place.

DEATH OF TWO YOUNG BOYS.

In 1867 there was a little settlement on Sandy composed of Moses Ball, C. B. Ball, Archie McDonald, James Green and Chesley Marlett. It was near this settlement that the Indians killed Brake Green and Billy Bailey, two boys of the settlement. The two boys went off together one Sunday morning, in the fall of 1867, to hunt for a pony that had strayed away. They expected to find him on Sandy Creek somewhere, so went in that direction. They were only about eighteen years old, and we can imagine them talking with each other of when fishing is good, where the best pecans and wild grapes grow; where to find the wild turkeys and the squirrels; occasionally casting furtive glances into the woods as they discuss in lower tones the probability of Indians being near-by. When about one-half mile from Mr. Green's house, suddenly right at them appeared a band of eleven Indians.

Shortly after this Archie McDonald was passing near there and found a small looking glass, squirrel skins and some red paint, and he knew the Indians were in the country. He did not know that the band had met the two boys. He turned back toward home and on to Mr. Ball's, where he reported what he had found.

Mr. C. B. Ball and Mr. J. Marlett, feeling certain that the boys had been overtaken by the Indians, started out to search for them. Sure enough, when the men reached Sandy Creek they found the dead bodies of the two boys. They had been horribly butchered. Appearances indicated that when the Indians surprised them both boys started to run. Young Green had run into the bed of the creek and was shot on the south bank, after he had crossed over. He was shot with three arrows. Two lodged in his breast and one in his back. When the two men found him his face was in the water. His pockets were turned wrong side out, and any money or valuables he might have had were taken. He was not scalped. Young Bailey was wounded before he got to the creek. He had stumbled along for about fifty yards, trying to get out of the way of the Indians. Indications showed that he had been cruelly tormented after they had scalped him. A wound in his arm seemed to have been made by a lance that had been thrust entirely through it. The Indians had shot him nineteen times. Mr. Ball and

Mr. Marlett were not sure that the Indians were not watching them when they found the bodies of the boys, but they tried to appear calm and indifferent. The sun was setting as they found them. It was impossible for the two men to carry the bodies home alone, and there was so much danger of being fired on from ambush by the Indians that they were forced to leave the bodies there until morning. The next morning kind hands bore them tenderly to their heartbroken parents. The coffins were made for them out of planks or boards, or anything they could use—material was so scarce and so far away.

Both boys were buried in the same grave. They were the first people ever buried in the "Selma Graveyard," which is only a few miles from Bowie. We are thankful that such days of anxiety and danger are over, and that the dreadful Indians will never trouble Montague County again. I have no doubt but what many of our boys have gathered pecans and walnuts and hunted squirrels near the same spot where these two boys met the band of Indians.

INDIANS KILL NATHAN LONG AND CAPTURE MISS PARALEE CARLTON.

In the fall of 1867 Nathan Long moved to what is known to old settlers as the "Chunky" Joe Wilson place, located four miles east of Forrestburg.

On January 5, following, known as Old Christmas, the Indians made a raid into Montague County. They committed a series of crimes that day and that night. The first was the killing of John Leatherwood. He was on his way home. When he reached Clear Creek he was killed by the Indians. After scalping him they left him there and went on down the creek to Nathan Long's place. On the way there they burned Charles McCracken's house to the ground. Passing on to the home of Wash and Alf Williams' they went through the house, robbing it of such things as they wanted. It was afterwards thought their reason for burning the McCracken home was because they found an Indian's scalp hanging in the house—a sight which always incited them to great fury. Their next move was to go to the Carlton home, situated in the Clear Creek Valley. Here they captured Miss Paralee Carlton, taking her with them.

Miss Carlton had an exciting experience. The Indians had a fight with the whites the night of the day she was captured. In the confusion following the flight of the Indians she managed to slip from her horse unnoticed by them. She laid down in the tall grass and remained in hiding until they were far on their way. The Indians drove the horses on, thinking she was along. Miss Carlton had walked about a mile, when she came to the home of Dr. Davidson, where she found refuge until she could be conducted to her home. Miss Carlton's nieces are teachers in the public schools of this county now.

The Indians next went to the home of Austin Perryman. They surrounded the house and prepared for an attack. At this point Mr. Perryman and his wife made a strategic move. Mrs. Perryman donned men's clothing, and thus attired assisted her husband in frightening them away. The Indians were in deadly terror of a gun in the hands of a white man, and they liked to know that they had the advantage before inviting an attack. By these maneuvers Mr. Perryman and his wife succeeded in causing the Indians to think there was a number of men in the house, so they departed without doing any harm.

The Indians were now going in the direction of Nathan Long's home. Mr. Long had been away from home on business. On this day he was returning home when overtaken by the Indians. He was unarmed, so could make no resistance. He made a desperate effort to escape by running his horse at full speed, hoping to reach home and protect himself and family. The Indians, divining his purpose, circled about him and cut off his approach to the house. They killed and scalped him. He was found by the neighbors next day and buried at the Elm Creek graveyard.

It was the custom among the settlers, when they

learned of the presence of Indians in the country, to send an "Indian runner" to warn the people. This was some brave white man, and it was not unusual for the settlers to hear these words as the runner paused for an instant on his fleetfooted horse: "Get your firearms and ammunition ready—the Indians are coming down the creek, killing and burning as they come." On he went, like the wind, to warn others. On the above occasion George Mason was warning the people, reaching the Long home just ahead of the Indians. Had he not done so, Mrs. Long and her children would have been killed or captured. She, together with her son and daughter, fled to the home of Mr. Wilbur, about one-half mile away, and escaped. The Indians visited their home and finding no one about, proceeded to a rent house on the same farm occupied by Chunky Joe Wilson and his children. Mrs. Long, in her flight with her own children, took time to go by and get the Wilson children and brought them with her. Had it not been for this, they would have been killed or captured. Finding no one at home here, the Indians contented themselevs with setting fire to the house and passed on, on their mission of slaughter and destruction. Miss Alice Wilson, the eldest daughter, had gone to church at Forrestburg that day and returned shortly after the Indians left to find her home in ashes.

On the same raid recounted above this same band

of Indians crossed into Cooke County, about two miles from the Montague County line. It was a clear, bright morning, such as nature often permits her Texas children to enjoy, even in the month of January. On this particular morning Mrs. Shegog, whose home was on Clear Creek, in the Roston neighborhood, was at home alone, with the exception of her baby, the two Menasco children and a little negro boy. We can imagine the children at play in the sunshine, while the good housewife, with a smile in her eye and snatches of song on her lips, is attending to her simple household duties. The baby laughs and crows, as only a dear little baby can. Everything looks peaceful and serene. Suddenly, without warning, the fiendish savages, with their dreaded war whoop, attack this lonely frontier home. They killed Mrs. Shegog's poor little baby in the most brutal manner in spite of the entreaties of the grief-stricken, terror-stricken mother. They then took Mrs. Shegog, the two Menasco children and the negro boy captive, and again started on their way. Mr. Menasco, Mrs. Shegog's father, had heard of the coming of the Indians, and was on his way to protect his daughter and grandchildren, when he, too, was killed by this same band.

As has been said before, it was a nice warm day, but with the sudden change peculiar to our Texas climate, it became bitterly cold toward night, and by midnight one of the worst blizzards known to this section was raging. It began sleeting and snowing, and the wind swept with terrific force across the bleak, open prairie.

The Indians were now traveling in the direction of Gainesville, in Cooke County. The Indians themselves were beginning to suffer from the cold. When within one mile of Gainesville, thinking Mrs. Shegog was frozen to death, the Indians threw her off on the ground and left her, as they supposed, dead. A large buffalo robe fell with her, and in this the poor, half frozen woman managed to wrap herself and laid on the bleak, open prairie until morning. At dawn she heard the chickens crowing, and made her way to the sound. It proved to be the home of Sam Dause. They gladly gave her food and shelter until an opportunity presented itself for her to return home. She did not know the fate of the children who were captured with her. It being night, and she, half unconscious from exposure to the bitter cold, did not see the Indians when they threw the little bodies on the prairie. They had frozen to death. Their fate was left to conjecture, until the following spring, when a party of cowboys, among them Mr. Charlie Grant, of near Forrestburg, discovered the remains of the children on the prairie.

The next morning after the capture and escape of Mrs. Shegog, the Indians again crossed over into Montague County. When about two miles from Forrestburg they killed four persons and captured two. Tom Fitzpatrick and his wife, Alice, were living near Forrestburg, on what is now known as the Ben Steadham place. They had two little girls and a baby boy. A runner, who had heard of the presence of this band of Indians in the country, went to warn the Fitzpatrick family of their danger. Mr. Fitzpatrick took his family and started at once for the home of Arthur Parkhill, a neighbor of theirs. He placed his wife and children on a horse, while he walked by their side. Arthur Parkhill, when he heard the Indians were coming, hurried to tell the Fitzpatricks about it that they might come to his home, where they could all be together for better protection from the Indians. He met them on the way and was returning with them when the little party of friends was surprised by the Indians. The Indians killed and scalped Mr. Parkhill and Mr. Fitzpatrick on the spot. This left the half distracted mother entirely unprotected and with three children on the horse with her. With all a mother's love she clung desperately to her little ones, and urged the horse forward with all of her might. The Indians were riding good horses and followed close behind her. "On, on, good horse," she cries. She reaches the gate of the picketed enclosure surrounding the Parkhill home. She takes fresh courage—safety lies so near. But, alas! before she could dismount and get inside the enclosure the Indians caught her. They killed and scalped her, killed the little baby and captured the two little girls. Nothing was learned of the fate of the two little girls for a long time. Finally they were found among the Indians of Western Kansas. Mr. Bud Morris of Montague assisted in the identification of the children. He had a lengthy correspondence with Colonel Leavenworth in regard to the matter. In the end Congress appropriated ten thousand dollars for their education and maintenance. Thus ended one of the bloodiest, most disastrous raids ever made in Montague County. The Indians passed out of the county, crossing Red River into the Indian Territory.

CAPTURE OF THE McELROY CHILDREN.

In the summer of 1868, Mr. Levi Perryman, a pioneer citizen and former sheriff of this county, was living with his family on what was known as the Foster Morris place. In June Mr. Perryman had been away on an eight-day cow hunt and barely escaped coming in contact with a band of Indians on his return home. There had been a light shower of rain the day of his return, and when he arrived home his wife told him that the rain had blown down his oats. He walked out to see what damage had been done, and while out there he saw his wife walk across the gallery with a gun and a pistol in her hands. The dogs were barking furiously, and he thought that Indians might be near the house. As he was hastening toward the house he was met by a little negro boy, who was frightened almost to death. His eyes were rolling as he said, "Massa Levi, Miss Josie said the Indians were killing Mr. McElroy's folks. Can't you hear them screaming?"

He hurried on to where his wife stood and asked her what was the matter. She replied, "The Indians are killing Mr. McElroy's folks. Can't you hear them screaming?"

Mr. Perryman ordered the negro to bring him a fresh horse. His wife asked him what he was going to do. When he told her he was going to the assistance of their neighbors she began to cry, fearing he would be killed by the Indians. But he went, anyway. He was riding a splendid horse, and soon reached the McElroy home. Mr. and Mrs. McElroy were in the front yard, screaming, "Oh, the Indians have stolen my children; my little children are gone, and we will never see them again." Their grief was terrible. Mr. Perryman asked which way the Indians went. They pointed out the way, and he was gone like a bird on the wing. The Indians had gone north, to where the "Stony Point" school house now stands. When Mr. Perryman reached this place he caught sight of the Indians in the distance. The children saw Mr. Perryman and recognized him. The children said afterwards that when they saw Mr.

Perryman they felt that they would be saved. But Mr. Perryman took the wrong trail and failed to rescue them. Instead, he followed the trail the Indians had made that morning. When he discovered his mistake it was too late to follow them further; so he decided to go on down Willa Walla Valley, and warn the people that the Indians were in the country.

The McElroy children were out gathering dewberries with a grown-up young man by the name of John Lackey, when they were attacked by the Indians.

They killed the man and captured the children. The father and mother, hearing the screams, ran out only to see the Indians disappearing in the distance with their two children, Nat and Dora Ellen. The Indians held the children captive on their reservation for quite a while. Their parents, who were making every effort to find them, finally learned of their whereabouts and bought them back through the government.

INDIANS CHARGE ON MR. JACKSON'S HOME ON DENTON CREEK.

In the fall of 1868 the families of Mr. Jackson and Rile Willingham were living together for protection from the Indians. About 4 o'clock one afternoon the two men, accompanied by Mr. Jackson's little boy, went to the well, which was some distance from the house. To please the little fellow they allowed him to ride the horse, which they were taking with them to water. Hearing a noise they looked up to see a band of Indians approaching the house. The Indians had a large number of horses with them, which was afterwards learned they had stolen in Denton County. There was no time to waste in discussing the situation if the men were to reach the house in time to protect their wives and children from being killed or captured by the Indians. They told the little boy to run the horse as fast as he could make him go, telling him if he hurried he could reach the house before the Indians and be saved. The two men, by cutting through a near way, reached the house first. Mr. Jackson saw an Indian aim at his little son as he came up on the horse. The frightened child was saved in an almost miraculous manner. He was running the horse with such speed that when he reached the fence surrounding the yard, the sudden stop threw the child over the horse's head into the yard. He ran into the house and was saved. The men hurriedly closed up both houses. Mr. Jackson had his family to get under the puncheon floor. He remained above, telling them if he was killed for them to stay under the floor and not to come out until every noise had ceased. He thought in that way they might be saved, provided the Indians did not burn the house.

From some cause the Indians decided not to molest the houses or their inmates, but contented themselves by taking all their horses, killing their hogs, shooting their cattle and burning their wheat and oat stacks. After they had destroyed nearly everything of any value in sight they fired a few shots and went on their way with the stolen horses.

INDIANS SLAY LIEUTENANT VAN ROBERTS.

There is no prettier spot in the whole of Montague County than where the town of Forrestburg stands. The soil is of a white waxy nature, and the roads in and about the town are perfect. Groups of live oak dotted here and there lend an air of beauty to the little town, and are especially beautiful in winter when the snow falls upon them, for they are evergreen in nature and remain green throughout the year. Near the edge of the town a little stream winds in and out and many picturesque spots are to be found near by. The wild grape vine flourishes here, the dogwood and wild plum blossoms are to be found along its banks in the springtime. There is one place in Forrestburg that is noted the country over; that is the Moore Hotel. Traveling men drive miles after dark to reach it, when they could easily find stopping places on the way. Lawyers, doctors, merchants and the public in general have enjoyed the hospitality and good cheer which pervades this splendid home.

If you ever have the good fortune to spend a few days in this quiet little town it will be hard for you to realize that it was once the center of war activities and Indian depredations. One Sunday in the fall of 1867 old Brother Descent, as he was familiarly called, was holding services at Forrestburg. Preaching services were few and far between, and the people were glad to attend them. A company of rangers stationed near Forrestburg, had taken advantage of the opportunity to listen to the preaching of the Word of God. They had just returned from church, and were unsaddling their horses, when some men came up and announced that a band of Indians had just captured the company's horses. Alec Frasier, who was described as being a remarkably handsome young fellow, jumped on his horse, without a saddle, and with gun in hand rushed out to where the Indians were and succeeded in getting all of the horses away from them except two of the finest ones. These the Indians were determined to keep. Young Frasier was riding a magnificent black horse. While he was rounding in the horses, Lieutenant Van Roberts ordered the rest of the company to resaddle their horses and start in pursuit of the Indians. They followed the Indians to (what is now) the business part of Forrestburg. At that time dense groups of live oaks were growing here and there in the street, making an excellent place from which to fight. The rangers caught up with the Indians at this point. When overtaken the Indians dismounted and got ready for battle; this was something very unusual for them, for an Indian always preferred to remain on his horse when fighting.

Lieutenant Roberts ordered his men to dismount, too. When the lieutenant and young Frasier dismounted the other rangers ran and left them. Several of the men were shot in the back by the Indians and afterwards died. The lieutenant said to his men: "For heaven's sake, boys, don't leave us like this." But they went on, anyway. This left Frasier and Roberts to battle with the Indians alone. They fought until their ammunition was exhausted. When they saw they could do no more, the lieutenant said: "Alec, we must get away from here." At the words Alec jumped on his powerful black horse, while Lieutenant Roberts attempted to mount his. The horse was a high spirited blue roan. He was already excited from hearing so many shots fired, and to add to his excitement an Indian kept waving a blanket in his face to frighten him. Every time the lieutenant would try to mount the Indian would wave the blanket, while another Indian would shoot him with an arrow. He tried to mount again and again. The last time he tried to get on, his horse jerked loose and ran off, leaving him on the ground. An Indian tried to jump on him, but he quickly got up, and with Bowie knife in hand ran the Indian until he fell. He arose and ran him three times, flourishing his Bowie knife as he ran. The last time he fell he was so weak from the loss of blood he couldn't get up, and the Indian scalped him alive. When an Indian scalped a white man who had exhibited great signs of bravery he only scalped a spot on the top of his head about the size of a dollar. Lieutenant Roberts was scalped in this way. This was evidence that the Indians regarded him as a brave man. Frasier ran for "Hegler's Store," which at this time was vacant. He took refuge here, expecting every moment that the Indians would surround him. They shot his hat off as he ran, and the next day the boys picked up eighteen arrows that the Indians had shot at him, none of them taking effect. After waiting for some time for the lieutenant to come he ventured forth with the hope of assisting him in some way. A strange quietness was all about. The sound of battle had ceased and the Indians had fled. Going to the spot he found his friend lying face downward—dead—his blood staining the grass on which he lay. Every opportunity after this his men would gather at this spot to pay a silent tribute to his bravery. For had it not been for the bravery of the two men the settlement might have suffered heavily at the hands of the Indian band. Today he is sleeping in the graveyard near

John McGee's. Often have the children been told of the bravery of Lieutenant Roberts and Alec Frasier.

The father of Lieutenant Roberts lived near Roberts' Spring, just a few miles from where the lieutenant was slain. The Indians, after killing him, went to this spring. Just before they reached there the three younger brothers of the lieutenant had been sent there to get water for the family use. They had an old five-gallon churn in which to get the water. They had dipped it nearly half full when the band of Indians surprised them. The boys ran as fast as possible, reaching home in a few minutes. In his excitement and fright, Rufus, the youngest boy, held on to the churn, carrying it with him in his flight. When they reached the house all three of the boys tried to talk at once. Rufus was still holding tight to the churn. His mother kept saying, "Rufus, put down that churn." But the boy was so badly frightened he just kept walking up and down the room, all the time holding the churn half filled with water, and saying, "I tell you we saw the Indians, mother; they like to have caught us, too. I tell you they did." At last they had to take the churn away from him by main force. His older brothers teased him about it a great deal afterwards, but he declared he was so badly frightened he didn't realize that he was holding the churn. Mr. Roberts and his son, George, took their guns and hurried to the spring and found the Indians were still there. Mr. Roberts shot one of the Indians, but as he was tied to his horse he did not fall off. This frightened the other Indians, and they fled, taking the wounded Indian with them. Soon after they returned to the house Captain Toddy and a company of rangers dashed up to the gate. The captain told Mr. Roberts that he had sad news for him; that the Indians had slain his son that day.

This was indeed sad news for the father and mother. The company of rangers pursued the Indians until they lost their trail, returning to quarters at Camp Brushy, two miles east of Forrestburg.

ANOTHER INDIAN RAID.

The month of March, 1867, is said by old settlers to have been one of the coldest periods ever known in this country. The "blue northers" for which this portion of Texas is noted, raged with unceasing fury, and thousands of cattle perished. The snow remained on the ground for more than twenty days. About the twenty-first of March, in this same year, a small band of Indians came into the county on foot. Their first act was to go to the home of Mr. Jimmy Waller, on Dye Creek. It was night when they reached there. Mr. Waller ran a sorghum mill and made molasses on shares for the entire neighborhood. His mill was near the bank of Dye Creek, so that he could obtain plenty of water. It happened at this time that he had on hand several barrels of molasses. The Indians were afraid to attack the house, and contented themselves with pulling the stoppers out of the barrels that held the sorghum, letting the contents run into the creek. It was jokingly said that Dye Creek ran with sorghum for a week afterwards.

The Indians then went on down Clear Creek to the home of John Carter, where they stole two horses from the stable, rounded up a bunch of prairie horses, mounted them and rode north across Elm Creek. On this same day Dan Brunson and John Short had started to Gainesville to mill, in a wagon drawn by slow moving oxen. Now, going to mill was no small matter in those days. The only mill in the country was an old-fashioned tread wheel mill, run by oxen. Besides the danger of being attacked by the Indians going and coming, they were likely to be detained there a week before their turn at the mill would come, as it was run on the plan of "first come, first served." The men had to take bedding and provisions with them when they went, not knowing how long they would have to wait.

Mr. Brunson and Mr. Short had not journeyed far until they were overtaken by the mail carrier. This "mail rider," as he was commonly called, was just a mere boy, but he carried the mail to and from Montague to Gainesville, across the bleak, open prairie, a courageous thing for a boy to do in those dangerous Indian times. In those days the majority of the people thought they were doing extremely well if they received mail every two or three weeks. What a contrast with today, for now the rural mail carrier passes their homes each day, except Sunday, to distribute the letters, magazines, papers and packages, and if anything happens that he cannot come, which seldom is the case, the people along his route are very much disappointed.

Let us return to our story. The three men were traveling slowly along when they were overtaken by Captain Brunson, the father of Dan Brunson. He had heard of the presence of the band of Indians in the country and feared they would come upon the men unawares. So he had come to warn them of the possible danger. They stopped and Dan Brunson borrowed the mail carrier's horse and went back to the head of Elm to get weapons with which to defend themselves in the event of their meeting the Indians. He rode like the wind, and when he had almost reached the wagon, on his return, he saw what he supposed to be the men he had left there, but instead he rode right into a band of Indians, who had surrounded the wagons. He called to the men. They had run into the brush at the approach of the Indians, and could hear him calling, but were afraid to answer him.

Mr. Brunson wheeled his horse about and rode back with all speed to the head of Elm. To his great surprise the Indians did not offer to follow him, although they saw him plainly. Instead, the Indians poured out all their corn and wheat and took their bedding, sacks and provisions. Mr. Brunson succeeded in getting up a party of men to assist in fighting the Indians. When they returned to the wagon, to their surprise, they met another party of men from Clear Creek, who were on the trail of the Indians. The Indians were now in sight, going north towards Red River. Mr. Charley Grant and others followed them to the brakes of Red River. One of the Indians went up on a mound to spy upon the movements of the white men. He saw some of the men turn back, but failed to see the others coming on, so after he reported, the Indians sat down to eat their dinner, as they supposed, in perfect safety. The white men surprised them, while they were grouped about eating, and would have killed a number, if not all, of them had not Henry Baine's gun gone off accidentally, giving the alarm. The Indians immediately gave fight, charging the men on foot. They wounded five horses. Three of them afterwards died. The fight began about 3 o'clock in the afternoon and continued until after dark. Not a white man was wounded. But there was evidence of some of the Indians being killed and wounded. In the thickest of the fray Kit King's horse ran under a tree and knocked him off. His horse ran toward the Indians. When the Indians saw him fall they thought they had killed him, and they gave their unearthly war whoop, and gobbled like turkeys. The men said Mr. King thought he was shot, too, at first, but when he found he was unhurt he made a dash for his horse. He succeeded in getting it back, and also one of the Indians' horses for Dan Brunson to ride, as his horse had been wounded in the battle, and was unable to carry him. After this the Indians withdrew and the white men returned to their homes.

INDIAN RAID NEAR SPANISH FORT.

In the early sixties Mr. A. Penton, with his family, was living near Spanish Fort, in this county. At this time the Indians had been raiding down on Denton Creek. It was the custom when they found the Indians had come over on the Texas side to send a runner to tell the people to head them off at the river crossing on their way to the Territory. At the time recorded Campbell Laforce came by Mr. Penton to warn him that the Indians were on the way, and wanted him to go and help overtake them. Laforce had ridden all night, but he lost no time in resting, but went on his way to warn others. Soon after he left Mr. Luther Landers came by and asked Mr. Penton to come and go with him to the Indian fight. He told him his horses were out, and he had nothing to ride. Mr. Landers said, "Well, let's walk out here to the edge of the prairie, and perhaps we may find your horses." They went on together, both carrying guns, Mr. Landers riding and Mr. Penton walking by his side. They reached a knoll called Herring's Point, and Mr. Penton looked down in the hollow and saw about eighteen Indians assembled there. They had nearly fifty horses with them. The Indians had seen the approach of the white men and had hidden there with the intention of surprising them. Mr. Landers and Mr. Penton held a council of war and decided to run. They started for the timber, knowing if they reached there they could better protect themselves from the Indians. Mr. Landers took Mr. Penton behind him on his horse, and they laughingly said afterwards that they tried to fly. In striking at his horse he struck Mr. Penton's gun. It went off and frightened the Indians away. They reached Mr. Penton's, and fearing the Indians would follow and attack the house they sent the entire family to a thicket at the back of the field and told them to remain there until all was over. About twenty-two white men came up about this time and charged the band of Indians. Among the men were Bill

Dixon, Eb Dixon, George Campbell, Burnett, Blair and a number of others whose names could not be obtained. The frightened women and children could hear the sound of the guns. This only served to increase their alarm, for they did not know what the result of the battle would be. Fortunately none of the white men were wounded, but a number of Indians were wounded. One Indian, whom they killed that day was old Chief Lone Wolf's son. The white men scalped him and his warriors left him where he fell, as it was contrary to Indian custom to carry a scalped Indian from the battlefield. Some of the Indians who succeeded in making their escape were riding some of Mr. Bill Freeman's fine race horses that they had stolen from him.

After the fight was over Mr. Penton brought his family to the house and they prepared dinner for the entire company of white men, twenty-two in number. The family considered it a privilege to dispense hospitality to these good pioneer men, who were always brave in the defense of the homes of Montague County.

INDIANS CAPTURE DICK FREEMAN AND JOHN BAILEY.

Perhaps the best known and most widely discussed "Indian capture" ever recorded in the history of Montague County was that of the capture of Dick Freeman and John Bailey.

The earliest home of Dick Freeman was in a rude log cabin just back of where the store at New Harp now stands.

One of the first accomplishments taught a boy in those days was how to manage a horse properly. Young Freeman soon became an expert horseman, and his father placed him in charge of a herd of cattle. He was as reliable as a man in looking after his father's interests. His father, Bill Freeman, owned a great many cattle, and his fine horses were known all over the county. In 1867 Dick Freeman and John Bailey, an orphan boy a little older than himself, to whom the family had given a home, were herding cattle on a small opening in the timber just east of their home, when they were surprised and taken captive by two Comanche Indians. John Bailey was riding a splendid horse that belonged to Jim Harry. The horse was known all over the county as "Billy Button." Many of the old settlers will remember him as a large red sorrel, sixteen hands high, with a white star in his forehead. (This is mentioned because that was a day when people really loved their horses.) The Indians passed within sight of the Freeman home with the boys. They could see the smoke curling peacefully from the chimney. "Let's take a last look at home, John, for we will never see it again," said

Dick, as he gazed longingly in that direction. He tried hard not to show any feeling, for the Indians usually punished any show of emotion; but in spite of everything a tear stole silently down the manly little fellow's cheek, and there was a choking sensation in his throat as he thought of the mother and father he would never see again.

They tied the two boys to a tree back of Levi Perryman's place, leaving an Indian to guard them, while the rest of the band went on to Mr. Perryman's house with the intention of stealing his horses. Mr. Perryman caught sight of the Indians, seized his gun and shot at them. This frightened them away. They returned to where the two captives were tied, placed them on horses and went on their way to the Comanche camp, in the Indian Territory. At first the two boys were treated most cruelly. They dragged them with ropes, caused them to walk barefooted in the snow, and allowed them to be tantalized in every conceivable manner by the Indian boys about the camp. At last Dick, who was a courageous little fellow, decided that he could never make his escape and would eventually be killed by the Indians, anyway, and he was going to teach one of those Indian boys a lesson. The time came when, soon after he had made up his mind, an Indian boy, much larger than Dick, began to tantalize him. The Indian was taken by surprise when Dick, with sudden fury, sprang upon him.

The Indian warriors began to circle around them, and Dick supposed his time had come at last. But he determined to give that Indian boy something to remember, and he redoubled his energies with increased vigor. He fairly rained blows upon the boy, scratching his face and tearing his hair, until the boy begged for mercy. Then Dick arose, folded his arms and looked his tormentors full in the face, expecting to be killed the next minute. Now, there is nothing in all the world that an Indian admires like bravery. To Dick's astonishment the Indians seized him, tossed him into the air, calling him "heap big warrior." From that time on he was a great favorite with the tribesmen. They taught him all sorts of Indian tricks, in riding, in lassoing, dancing and swimming. He remained with them nearly a year, and could speak the Comanche language fluently.

On the day the boys were taken captive, when the time came for them to return home, their failure to appear caused the family much alarm. A searching party went to look for them, and when they found Dick's saddle that had been dropped by the way, they were convinced that the boys had been killed by the Indians and were given up for dead. When nearly a year had passed by some citizens were in the vicinity of the Comanche camp, in the Indian Territory, when they unexpectedly saw and recognized John Bailey. They bought him from the

Indians and brought him home. He had not been in the same camp with Dick and could not say whether Dick had been killed or not. His return aroused a renewed hope within the father's heart that would not be stilled. He determined to make an effort to recover his son. Mr. Freeman armed himself heavily, mounted his finest horse and, accompanied by a brave friend, he rode to the Indian camp on the Washita River. To his great joy he found Dick alive and well, but to all outward appearances he was an Indian. The Indian chief had become so fond of him he had tried in every way to cause him to forget all he knew about civilization.

He had discarded his clothes for the Indian garb. They had allowed his hair to grow long, had painted his face Indian fashion and caused him to wear rings in his ears and bracelets on his arms, and carefully taught him the Comanche language. In spite of all this Dick recognized his father at first sight, ran to him and begged him to take him back to mother and the children. The Indians had formed such an attachment for the boy it was with great difficulty that they were induced to give him up. At last Freeman offered them the fine horse he was riding and five hundred dollars in money, and they consented to give him up. The Indians took a great dislike to Mr. Freeman, and told him if they ever caught him out anywhere in after years that they would kill and scalp him. To demonstrate the manner of death they meant they passed their knives about his head. There was great joy in the Freeman household when the father returned with Dick. The neighbors gathered in to see the boy that had been stolen, and to hear him relate his experiences with the Indians. His Indian antics and Comanche language amused the boys very much. Gradually he dropped the Indian customs he had acquired, and it finally became almost impossible to induce him to speak of his captivity. Not far from where he was captured this boy, now grown to manhood, lives in a pretty white cottage at the foot of a high hill. It is a beautiful spot, and from the front porch a magnificent view is to be had of the country, over which the Indian was wont to roam in the long ago. The father of John Bailey, who is spoken of in this story, lived in Wise County, at the home of Jim Ball. One day Mr. Ball was in his field when he suddenly beheld a large band of Indians coming down the mountain side. They ran by him on to where Tom Bailey was at work. Mr. Ball's little son was with him at this time. An Indian attempted to capture the child, and succeeded in getting him up behind him on the horse, when Bailey shot him in the forehead. The Indian fell forward, and the child slipped to the ground. Another Indian killed Bailey and captured the child. He was afterwards bought back by his father. A long time afterwards the Indians passed through that section of the country and were pursued by a band of white men. The Indians managed to escape, but had to leave one of the Indian ponies behind that had given out in the race and could run no further. The men brought the pony back with them and stopped at Mr. Ball's house. The little boy came out clapping his hands with joy as he exclaimed, "Old Hal has sent me my pony. He has seven holes in his ears to put ribbons in." The men examined the pony's ears and found what the child had said to be true, and gave the pony to him. When the little boy was a captive in an Indian camp he became a great favorite with old Chief Hal, and he had given him this pony to ride so long as he remained on the Indian reservation. The Indians frequently became very much attached to the white children whom they captured, and could scarcely be induced to give them up.

THE LOST SOLDIER.

In the winter of 1868 a scouting party was sent out from Fort Sill. On their way they camped at different places. One night they hobbled their horses and turned them loose to graze. Next morning was foggy and misty. In looking for the horses one of the soldiers became separated from his companions, and was not seen by them again for several months. They searched for him for a while, but concluding that he would join them later they went on their way, leaving him to his fate. He had a terrible experience. Left without food and but little ammunition, he scarcely knew what to do. For days he traveled through the woods, afraid to shout or fire his gun, for fear he would attract the Indians. Finally, becoming desperate from hunger, he killed game to live on as long as his ammunition lasted. After that was exhausted he took the magazine out of his gun to make fish hooks with which to catch fish. As a last resort he was forced to kill his horse for food. He spent a week drying the horse flesh. During this time he took off his army blouse and tied it to a pole. He then climbed the highest cottonwood tree he could find and tied it in the top, hoping some one would see it in passing and come to his assistance. After waiting several days he became discouraged and decided to start out again through this strange country in an effort to find civilization. He was beset with many dangers. Besides the great loneliness of the woods, and the certain knowledge that he was lost, was his almost starving condition, and his fear of the Indians. Finally the desire for the sight of a human face became so strong that he lost all fear of the Indians, and would gladly have welcomed the sight of one. He took the precaution to take the mane of his horse and made a wig to wear, so if he was seen by

Indians they would mistake him for one of their own race, and they would not kill him at first sight.

The lower part of his boots, by this time, were completely worn out by constant walking over rough places, so he took the tops of the boots, together with pieces of horse hide, and made moccasins with which to protect his tired, worn feet. His clothing was worn and torn. His hair and beard long and unkempt. It only goes to prove how sparsely the country was settled, when it is known that he wandered for three months without having seen a human face, not even an Indian. He said that he prayed earnestly, time and again. At last he prayed the Almighty to give him some sign to cheer him if he was ever to be found at all. He declared that a great light shone about him, and he was greatly comforted.

It was now April. Cash McDonald and Bob Stephens of Montague County had started out to overtake a herd of cattle that had passed through their settlement, and see if any of the neighbors' cattle were in the herd. They crossed over into Clay County and that night, when near Buffalo Springs, they came upon a small hackberry thicket and saw the faint glimmer of a light. Their first thought was that it was an Indian camp fire, and they held a council as to what they should do. They decided to call and see what the result would be. At the sound of their voices the man ran out to meet them.

He was overcome with joy, talking and crying at the same time. He said repeatedly, "Thank God for a white man's face once more." The only provisions he had with him was some dried horse flesh. After listening to the story of his three months' wanderings they divided their food with him and told him to camp there until morning, when they would return for him.

He feared that they were only taking this method to get rid of him, and after they left he followed down the road in the direction the men had taken. The next day the men met him on the way. They took it time about riding and walking. They made such slow progress in this way that Mr. Stephens told him to camp for the night and he would send a boy back with an extra horse for him next day. The man was so anxious to reach civilization he attempted to walk on, and was met next day by Hiram Wainscot and taken to Queen's Peak. At this time Mr. Stephens had charge of Solen Loving's cattle at Queen's Peak, and had a number of cowboys working for him. He took the lost man in and clothed him. Finding him to be a fine cook he employed him to do the cooking for himself and the cowboys. A company of soldiers was stationed at Jacksboro. The man reported to them, and they reported to his company at Fort Sill. By this means he communicated with his company and afterwards returned to them. His gratitude toward the men who found him knew no bounds. He frequently wrote to Hiram Wainscot, to whom he was greatly attached.

AMONG OTHER INDIAN CRUELTIES.

Mr. Stump, a citizen of Montague County, living near Clear Creek, accompanied by a young man named Bailey, who worked for him on the farm, had started to Sherman to mill. They did not feel any special fear of Indians that morning, as there had been no raids through that part of the county in some time. There had been a number of small hunting parties, composed of Indians, passing through the country, but they had appeared disposed to be friendly, although they would steal the settlers' horses whenever opportunity afforded. It never paid to feel too secure from danger in Indian times, for when you least expected them the foe was upon you. Mr. Stump, although urged by his family to take his fire arms with him, would not do so, saying he would leave them for the protection of the family, and that he was not apprehensive of danger anyway on this trip.

The men had traveled about a quarter of a mile from home when they suddenly came upon a band of Indians. The Indians at once surrounded them, and young Bailey began to cry, saying he knew they were going to kill them. The Indians told them to have no fears, that they were good, friendly Caddos. After a short conversation the Indians began shooting. They stopped as suddenly as they began, and forced the men to remove their clothing. They began shooting again, killing young Bailey instantly. This killing took place near where the "Peabody school house" now stands. When he saw young Bailey fall, Mr. Stump made a dash to escape, with two Indians in pursuit. He was a swift runner, but as he ran the Indians' bullets pierced him in more than a dozen places. He left the road and started to run through the woods. This gave him some advantage, for the Indians were riding horses and could not make fast progress through the undergrowth. Mr. Stump ran about four hundred yards, when he saw a man at work in a field near-by. He crossed over to him and fell at his side. The man's name was Priest. According to pioneer custom, Mr. Priest had his gun with him in the field. With it he succeeded in frightening the Indians away. He then turned his attention to the wounded man. He was unable to walk, and Mr. Priest could not carry him without assistance, so there was nothing else to do but leave him there and go for assistance. It was a trying moment for Mr. Stump, to be left there wounded, helpless and with nothing to defend himself with, not knowing what minute the Indians would return and scalp him. Fortunately this did not happen, and in a short time Mr. Priest returned with help, and they carried the wounded man to the Priest home. He remained there a month, when, in spite of his dangerous wounds, he was nursed back to health and strength, and in 1912 was still alive.

AN INDIAN ATTACK.

The Indians, when raiding through the county, came down near a place called the "Old Music Farm." A widow by the name of Davis lived there, together with several children. Her oldest daughter was called Nan. Late one evening they heard horse bells down at the creek near-by, and thinking their horses had come up for water, Nan and her mother started out to catch them, and bring them to the house. When they reached the creek they saw a band of Indians there. The Indians discovered their presence about the same time and made an attempt to capture them. They did not seem inclined to kill them, but were determined to capture Nan. The girl fought desperately, but finally one of the Indians succeeded in getting her behind him on his horse. She managed to get down and ran through the briars and undergrowth until she reached the Hamilton home, quite a distance away.

Her clothing was torn and her hands and feet were torn and bleeding from contact with the sharp briars. The Indians had a large bunch of horses they had stolen, and rather than run the risk of losing them they let her go, and did not try to follow. The mother ran away while they were fighting with Nan. She hurried home to her other children and barricaded the house, but the Indians went another route, and they were safe.

QUEEN'S PEAK INCIDENT.

Indian depredations had become so frequent that three families had become alarmed for their safety and decided to live together for protection from the Indians.

They were Rile Willingham and family, R. J. Sandifer and family, and Mrs. Chesley Marlett and family. They were living in a cattle corral at Queen's Peak. One morning they heard some shooting in the distance. Looking out they saw the Indians killing and scalping two negroes who were on their way to the fort when overtaken by the Indians. After killing the negroes the Indians divided into two companies. They had about twenty-eight loose horses feeding near-by. One company of Indians stayed with the horses. The others climbed on top of the Peak so that they could look down into the corral and discover how many men were there. They seemed to tire of this and contented themselves with shooting down fourteen head of cattle. Then they began to maneuver again to find out the number of men in the corral. Rile Willingham and Lonnie Stephens were the only men there. Mrs. Sandifer and Mrs. Willingham dressed to represent men and completely fooled the Indians. They put all the little children down in a little dugout for protection. Mrs. Marlett, who held a gun, was asked if there was any more ammunition. She answered no. Her house was in the same enclosure, so she said she would go and get some ammunition that was there. They tried to keep her from going, but she said, "What can we do without ammunition if the Indians attack us?" She crossed over to her house and got the ammunition. An Indian, who was on a horse and heavily armed, looked straight at her as she came out, but made no effort to harm her. It was supposed he refrained from killing her because he feared an attack from the men on the inside, and being uncertain as to their number he hesitated about firing. She secured the ammunition and returned unhurt.

After riding around near the corral for almost two hours the Indians left. For a while they feared they would return, but the Indians decided not to molest them further, and they were left in peace for a while.

Immediately following the Queen's Peak affair Frank Marlett, Mount Stroud, Dick Sandifer, Joe Johnson and Bud Leath had gone to the Green place, about one mile distant from the Marlett home. When nearly half way back home they suddenly came upon a band of Indians. At first they thought they were cowmen, but when they discovered they were Indians they made their way to a hollow near-by and prepared for a fight. A few shots were exchanged, but no one was hurt. It was the purpose of the Indians to steal the horses at the Marlett place belonging to the men, and when they found this was impossible they passed over the ridge and out of sight.

OLD TIP'S DISLIKE FOR THE INDIANS.

In the early days of this county no possession was more highly appreciated than a good horse. A swift horse was known by name all over the settlement, and to own one was a very good introduction to public favor. For a good judge of horseflesh was held in no slight esteem.

Many a man owed his escape from the Indians to his fleetfooted horse. As a rule they were keenly alive to Indian signs, and their restless manner and other exhibitions of uneasiness would often warn their masters of danger when they least expected that Indians were near. These instincts were characteristic of "Old Tip." He possessed the true pioneer spirit in that he shared the pioneer's dislike for the Indian. He was fleet of foot and strong of limb.

He was devoted to his master, and made his way back to him on different trying occasions. His large eyes looked out upon the world with intelligent interest. Old Tip was a horse and his master's name was Sam McDonald. Mr. McDonald and his family were living with his father, Cash McDonald, and family, on Denton Creek. They lived in separate houses, but within the same enclosure, for protection from the Indians. The doors to this enclosure opened on the inside, giving the occupants some advantage over the Indians. They had also picketed in a space for the horses. It was within this picketed space that "Old Tip," together with the other horses belonging to the family, was wont to spend his nights. He stood in mortal terror of the Indians, and when his master heard him pawing and snorting at night this was warning enough. He knew that "Old Tip" had discovered that Indians were near. In the summer of 1867 the Indians made a raid on the McDonald home at night. John Wainscot and his son, Isaac, were spending the night with the family. Mr. McDonald was awakened by Old Tip pawing and snorting. Feeling certain that Indians were near he got up to investigate. A white tablecloth had been hung over the door that day, and as Mr. McDonald opened the door to look out, an Indian, that had been stationed to watch the house, saw the cloth and, mistaking it for a man, fired. The bullet failed to strike Mr. McDonald, lodging in a post at the side of the picket. The shot aroused the other members of the family. In the confusion that followed the Indians succeeded in getting Old Tip and a fine mare and colt. The men could see the Indians in the bright moonlight, crossing the field, and recognized the horse they had stolen. A few shots were exchanged, but to no effect. "Old Tip" managed to get away from the Indians next day and came back home. The other horses were never recovered.

On another occasion Old Tip was hobbled. He was grazing peacefully when suddenly his instinct warned him that the Indians were near. Instantly he started to flee. The Indians made every effort to capture him. They ran him several miles. The horse was wise enough to try to reach the fort. Finally the Indians succeeded in getting a lariat on him. It took one Indian to manage him while the other Indians were exchanging shots with Isom McDonald, Dace McDonald and Fred Broadstreet, who had seen the capture of the horse and started in hot pursuit. The Indians, seeing that the fight would prove disastrous to themselves were forced to turn Old Tip loose and run. The next day "Old Tip" was found by the men. He was badly bruised by the hobbles. In his course he ran by where the Dry Valley church now stands, on across to what is now known as the Holbrook farm. Sam McDonald slipped up and caught hold of the lariat and wrapped it around a tree. He had some difficulty in approaching the horse because the rope had the scent of Indians on it. By persistent patting and coaxing he finally managed to reassure "Old Tip" that he was in the hands of friends. His master said: "Old fellow, you have made good your escape from the Indians again, and as long as I own you, you shall never wear hobbles again." And "Old Tip." was exempt from hobbles from that day.

INDIANS DISTURB PREACHING SERVICE.

Rev. Joe Weaver was holding a protracted meeting at Hegler's Store (now called Forrestburg). Most of the people of the settlement had availed themselves of the opportunity to attend these services. Mrs. McCracken, a good pioneer Christian woman of the neighborhood, had not been situated so that she could attend the meeting, so she sent word to the minister to announce that if he would come and hold one service at her home on Sunday she would prepare dinner for all who would come. Quite a number accepted the invitation. After the service was over and dinner had been served the people began to leave. The minister was one of the first to go, as he had announced services for that afternoon. Some of the party lingered for a while, going on later to the meeting. On their way they caught sight of an Indian spy in the distance. A little further on they saw about forty Indians assembled. By this time the congregation had arrived and the singing was in progress. A Mr. Southward went to the minister and whispered to him of what he had seen. The minister announced this to the congregation, at the same time advising the men to put the women and children in the store for protection, while the men stood guard on the outside. This announcement instantly changed the service into war preparations, every man holding a gun in his hand ready for action. All of the congregation remained there except Joe and Milo Box, their sister, Pink, Mr. Southward and his pretty daughter, Lou (who afterwards became Mrs. Joe Box), and the Rev. Mr. Weaver. Their mother had remained at home that day and the Box children, fearful that the Indians might attack their lonely cabin home, refused to remain in comparative safety while Mrs. Box was threatened with danger. From some unknown cause the Indians decided to leave the county without molesting the settlers, but they succeeded in breaking up a good meeting.

They traveled southeast into Denton County, pursued by a band of rangers from Montague County. When the Indians caught sight of the rangers they broke and ran as if they were badly frightened. This proved to be only a ruse to get the soldiers to follow them. The soldiers quickly rode after them, to find that the greater number of the Indians had secreted themselves in the grass and began firing at them as they rode up. The Indians now began to circle around them, Indian fashion. Sergeant Cobb said, "Boys, there has got to be some fighting done. Dismount and make breastworks of your horses."

The soldiers then opened fire on the Indians, but without result. In the meantime the Indians were circling closer and closer to them. A boy of sixteen was one of the company. His mother had died some time before this and he had no place to stay, so his father, who belonged to the rangers, took him everywhere he went. The boy was riding the finest horse in the company and was a plucky little Indian fighter, and was a great favorite with the company.

In the thickest of the fray he was wounded by a shot from an Indian. He called out, "Father, I'm wounded." The father knew it was no time to sympathize with him and, although much alarmed about his condition, he smiled bravely as he replied, "It can't be helped, son, kill an Indian." Thus encouraged, the little fellow held out bravely for a while, but soon began to grow faint from loss of blood.

The rangers' horses were so tired from being ridden so far that they scarcely moved, although the bullets fell thick and fast about them.

Sergeant Cobb ordered: "Boys, every man take deadly aim at the front Indians." When the smoke cleared away they discovered they had killed the

Indian chief. He was tied on his horse, and after he was killed the horse he was riding ran into the rangers' ranks and was captured. The horse was a beautiful gray that the Indians had stolen from Bart Trailer. The Indians had painted flowers and curious designs all over him. The Indians became confused, just as they always did when their chief was slain. They were falling fast under the deadly fire of the rangers.

Sergeant Cobb now said: "We must retreat; our boy can't hold out much longer." And indeed, by now, the little fellow was almost in a fainting condition. "Retreat in an orderly manner," was the command. As they were obeying his command one of the rangers saw an Indian just in the act of killing him with a long spear. He shot the Indian through the forehead, and his horse began to kick and plunge. The Indian was tied on, and the last the rangers saw of the Indian was his foot sticking up in the air as, tied to his horse, he went over the hill. This amused the wounded boy, who could not help but smile as he saw the Indian's foot high in the air, disappearing in the distance.

The company took the boy to the home of a man near by, where he remained until morning. His condition was much improved by the next day, and the entire company rode back to their camp at the old Austin Morris place, north of where Levi Perryman now lives, near Forrestburg. The boy was the only one of the company who was wounded.

INDIAN SKIRMISH BETWEEN CENTRALIA AND DYE MOUND.

Mr. Bud Morris of Montague and Mr. Holloway Williams were riding leisurely along one day when they suddenly rode up on ten Indians, near Dye Mound. They drove the Indians into a ravine, after shooting one Indian off his horse. They left the Indians in the ravine and went to Montague after recruits. They returned with the men, and the Indians, who had remained in the ravine, began firing on them. Mr. Morris was shot through his clothing with an arrow, but it failed to touch him. Mr. Williams was shot through his clothing, but they failed to wound him. Mr. Perryman's horse was wounded but afterwards recovered. Mr. Perryman was the only man in the company that was hurt. He sustained a slight injury on the temple, made by a flying bullet. The white men killed four Indians and wounded others. They also captured all of the Indians' horses but one. The Indians ran off on foot.

A PIONEER WOMAN'S EXPERIENCE WITH THE INDIANS.

While it has been impossible to give an account of all the Indian depredations in Montague County yet the following story will serve to show the harrowing experiences endured by nearly every pioneer woman of this county. It would be hard to find a woman who lived in those days that has not at least been badly frightened by the Indians. If the Indians failed to appear they were in constant dread for fear they would. Mrs. Levi Blankenship, who has been living two and one-half miles east of Forrestburg ever since 1861, said that she suffered much uneasiness for fear the Indians would attack her home in the absence of her husband. Her father enlisted in the Southern army soon after they moved into the county. She said that she well remembered with what sad hearts the wives and mothers gathered about a large log heap fire built near Hegler's Store (now called Forrestburg) on a cold, dreary morning, to bid farewell to husbands, sons, and fathers. How proudly the little company marched around and around the store. Then the good-byes were said. Some went to return and others fell on the field of battle.

About twenty-five Indians passed her house one morning. Four of them came near her door and motioned for her to come and go with them. She shook her head at them, and one of the Indians shot at her. She bravely said, "I can shoot, too," and went in the house to get a gun. They stole her horses and passed on. She then took her children and fled to the woods with them. Later her husband, who had returned home, came and called her, and they went to the home of her father, Mr. Ben Steadham. Here they found that the Indians had attacked the Steadham home that day, and Mrs. Steadham had donned a man's hat and took a gun and frightened them away.

Mr. Blankenship frequently went as an Indian runner to warn the people of the presence of Indians.

DEATH OF ANDY POWERS.

In October, 1866, Andy Powers, a citizen of Montague County, whose home was on Clear Creek, was traveling with a companion, whose name could not be learned, from Gainesville to Forrestburg. On the way they were attacked by a band of Indians. Powers' companion was riding a fine horse, and when they saw the Indians approaching he tried to get him to leave the mule he was riding and get up behind him, and they would outrun the Indians. This Powers refused to do. The poor man had a chill at the time and was quite sick. His companion said afterward that he did not seem disposed to make much resistance. The man seeing they would be overpowered and killed, and being unable to persuade Mr. Powers to come with him, fired one shot at the Indians and fled. They killed and scalped Andy Powers, leaving him on the spot, but taking his scalp and all valuables that he had with him.

"INDIAN CUNNING."

In the spring of 1870 a group of men were at the home of John Willingham on Denton Creek, near Denver, shoeing their horses. Andy Jackson had turned his horse loose, with the bridle and saddle on it, to graze around for a while. He looked at the horse occasionally, but as proof of the daring and adventure of the Indian, while the attention of the men was directed for a few minutes to the work in progress, an Indian slipped up unobserved and stole the horse. Rile Willingham went to look for the horse and saw the Indians disappearing over the ridge with four horses belonging to the men assembled there. They were all good horses, for a fine horse was the pride of the sturdy pioneer's heart. They could plainly see Isaac Wainscot's horse grazing in the valley. Andy Jackson ran to where he was, took the hobbles off the horse and got on bareback, riding like the wind to the home of John Wainscot. He saw Cash Wainscot plowing steers in the field near by. He called to the men in the field to get their horses and come on, that the Indians were in; then rushed on his way to warn others. He started to where a crowd of men were herding cattle, to warn them of the danger of being surrounded by the Indians. When he got to the corner of what is now known as Grisom's field he paused to look back, and found that the Indians were following him. Realizing his danger he turned to run. He knew the speed of his horse, and felt that the Indians were gaining on him all the time. He came over the hill, riding straight for John Wainscot's. Some men were at work in a field near by and saw him coming. Mr. Bob Savage, who was one of the men, called out, "Come on, boys." This frightened the Indians away.

The Indians now rode in the direction of Dry Valley, stealing horses from Fred Broadstreet, Marsellus Broadstreet and Charlie Jones. They passed on to the Freeman place. Here they stole Mose Johnson's fine race horse, "Old Yellow Boy." Ike Wainscot and Cash McDonald followed the Indians for nearly a mile. The Indians had left a horse in their hurry, and the McDonald boys went out to catch it. Jarrold McDonald, father of Cash, stayed back on the hill to watch and see if the Indians charged the boys. The boys secured the horse and returned to their father. Here a most laughable (but at the time serious) thing happened. Dean McDonald, with ten or twelve other men, was herding cattle near by. It took very little to make a man look like an Indian in those days, and many laughable mistakes were made. So when Dean McDonald saw the men on the hill in the distance he took them to be Indians. He showed them to the other men and they all, with one accord, made a hurried departure for camp

Those who had remained at camp saw them coming, and believing them to be Indians began to make preparations for war. Those on the hill saw the first group running, and thinking they had seen the Indians coming around the hill they at once rode at full speed in their direction. Those in front looked back, still believing their pursuers to be Indians. They put spurs to their horses and renewed the race with increased vigor. One of the party glanced back and said, "Boys, I see a rusty old Indian there in front, and he is ready to fight."

Finally when all parties reached camp, and they discovered that they had mistaken friends for enemies; explanations followed and they indulged in a hearty laugh, for that was the last seen of that band of Indians.

BROTHER AND SISTER DEFEND THEIR MOTHER'S HOME FROM THE INDIANS.

On a certain morning in the fall of the year Mr. Joe Box (who now lives near Forrestburg) and his brother, Milo, were going over to a neighbor's (Mr. Keenan) to help gather corn. The Box family at this time were living about five miles from Forrestburg. Before leaving home that morning Joe, the oldest brother, called his little ten-year-old brother to him and said, "Cal, we are going to be gone today and I am going to leave mother and the girls in your care. If the Indians come while we are gone I want you to defend mother." With true pioneer spirit Cal replied that he would. Joe loaded the rifle and placed it on the rack, ready for use.

As the brothers waved good bye to the little fellow he walked into the house, his heart swelling with pride to think his brother would give him such an important charge. In the afternoon Cal was looking out the door, when he discovered some Indians in the corn patch near by, trying to steal his mother's horses. The family had just been talking of how bravely Mrs. Trailor and her daughters had defended themselves from an Indian attack, when Cal said, in an excited tone, "Mother, I see Indians in the corn patch." His mother, thinking his remark was the result of an overwrought imagination, said, "Oh, you are joking, Cal." "No, I'm not, mother," he said, as he climbed up on a chair and took the gun from the rack.

By this time the mother's fears were thoroughly aroused, and looking out she saw several Indians near the house. Cal stepped out in the yard and drew his gun on the Indians. The Indians were wearing shields on their arms, which they held between them and Cal's gun. Fortunately the trigger of his gun failed to work, for if he had fired at the Indians they would probably have killed him. His sister, Belle, took down another rifle and coming out took her stand by her little brother's side. (Belle was only 12 years old.) Afterwards Cal said "Sister was calm and brave, but her smile helped me more than anything else." (This little girl is now Mrs. Ben Steadham of Forrestburg.) Mrs. Box, the mother of the two children, was in the house, screaming with fright. In the house with her was her little daughter, Pink, 8 years old. This child had presence of mind enough to close and fasten the door. Poor Mrs. Box was so uneasy about the two children on the outside that she jumped up and down, looking through a crack in the house, until she rubbed all the skin off her nose. This amused the children very much after the danger had passed and they were told how it happened. The Indians did not attempt to molest the family. Their main object seemed to be to steal the horses before any men arrived. They finally succeeded in driving the horses out of the field, taking them with them. Although Mrs. Box knew they would feel the loss of their horses keenly, she was thankful that their lives had been spared.

Later Mr. Crede Roberts passed the house and Mrs. Box asked him to go and tell her sons of the occurrence. They came home at once. Joe Box and Mr. Roberts followed the Indians until after dark. It began raining so hard that they had to hold their hats over their guns to keep the caps and powder dry. They decided it was best to return home, as they were in great danger of being surrounded by the Indians in the fast gathering darkness. Mr. Box recovered his stolen horses in about one month. It happened in this way: The Indians were in deadly terror of the infantry. They called them "Walk a Heap." This band of Indians who had stolen the Box horses ran into a company of soldiers. The soldiers were scouting for Indians when they were surprised by this band. The Indians fled, leaving some of the horses, but next day, fearing the long range guns of the soldiers, they abandoned the entire herd and went on foot through the mountains, hoping in this way to avoid the soldiers. The soldiers went through the town of Montague with the captured horses. Mr. Wayburn, the first sheriff of Montague County, Colonel Maynes and Uncle Johnnie Morris recognized the brands on the Box horses and went to Captain Erwin and told him to whom the horses belonged. The captain said: "If the parties owning the horses will be in Montague County on a certain Saturday they can have the horses." When Saturday came Joe Box went to Montague to claim his horses. When he arrived there he found the captain gone, and learned that he had refused, at the last, to give up the horses, saying he was going to sell them. The injustice of such an action made Joe very indignant, and he told the sheriff if his brothers came there looking for him to tell them he had started after the soldiers, and not to look for him until they saw him coming.

Joe followed the trail of the soldiers until night. Not being much more than a mere boy, he began to get very lonesome, with nothing to eat, no place to sleep and no lariat to tie his horse with. When it began to get dark he skylighted a man on a high ridge in front of him on a horse. Knowing that if he were an Indian he would be likely to get him anyway, and if he were a white man, he wanted to see him, Joe rode on toward him. In approaching the man he discovered a band of men, who had stopped in a valley near by. He didn't know whether they were Indians or not, but he had lost the soldiers' trail, and he decided to go to them, as he felt sure they had already seen him. As he drew near he could see a tent and heard a man say, "I guess that is the man who owns these horses." Sure enough, the men proved to be the soldiers he had been following all day. He rode up to the camp and told the men why he was there, at the same time describing the brand of his horses. One of the soldiers said, "We have them." They asked him if his horse was not tired, and invited him to get down and rest. Joe asked one of the soldiers to tell Captain Erwin he was there, why he had come and that he would like to see him.

The captain sent him word that he was engaged in a game of cards and couldn't see him until morning, but to issue him rations, give him a bed and take care of his horse. Joe slept with a soldier that night, using his saddle for a pillow and with the stake rope at his head.

In the night Joe heard his horse snort. Being a Spanish horse he was a splendid guard. Joe peeped from under his blanket and saw a man standing between him and his horse. He looked first at Joe and then at the horse and cautiously picked up the rope with the intention of leading the horse away. Joe raised up with gun in hand. The man hastily dropped the rope and ran off through a lake of water near by, splashing the water as he went. Joe was never sure whether the man was an Indian or not. He did not arouse anyone, but again lay down upon his pallet. The next day was Sunday. After breakfast Joe held a conversation with Captain Erwin. He told him how anxious his mother must be at his continued absence, and how badly they needed their horses at home. He then asked permission to take his horses and go. After listening to his story, the captain said: "I sympathize with your mother, but I have let one of my men ride one of your horses. I can't set him down here on foot. If you will go with me to headquarters I'll turn the horses over to you."

He ordered his men to mount. The next order was to march. There was nothing left for Joe to do but go with them. They reached headquarters that day, and Joe remained with them until the next morning.

The horses were turned over to him free of charge. He had his horse saddled by daylight and ready to start. He waited for the sun to rise before starting, so that he would know which direction to take. There were no roads, and he had never been in that part of the country before, and he had to take the sun as a guide. The soldiers gave him a lunch to take with him, but he never stopped to eat it until he reached Queen's Peak, which was at sundown. Hastily eating it he started on to Montague, ten miles away.

Joe had one little scare that day. He had seen what he took to be a band of Indians. He thought they were traveling like they intended to meet him. There was no choice in the matter, so he went on. But he had his trusty rifle ready to fire. When he reached the creek where he first saw them he failed to find any Indian signs, so he concluded it was a herd of buffalo that he had seen. When Joe reached Montague he heard from home. Some of the neighbors were there attending district court. They told him his mother and family were well and tried to get him to stay all night, but he said, "No, I must see mother before I sleep." After resting his horses for a while he started for home. He reached home at 1 o'clock that night, having ridden nearly one hundred miles. He found his mother walking the yard, consumed with anxiety and grief over her absent boy. She clasped him to her breast, as she wept tears of joy over his return. The little children heard her and they came out to add their joyous welcome to hers.

His mother told him that they had decided that he had been killed by the Indians, and that his brother, Milo, was out then with a party of friends searching for him. When she told him this Joe fired two shots from his gun, which sounded long and loud. This was to let the searching party know that he had returned.

After he had put up the horses he went into the house and found his mother preparing him a good hot supper. He said, "Why, mother, I didn't want you to cook supper for me at this hour of the night." His mother laid her hand tenderly on his head as she said, in tender tones, "Nothing is too good for my boy." When the meal was ready the family gathered around the table, each one striving to pass him something, while they plied him with questions about his trip.

The mother shuddered as she thought of the many dangers that could have overtaken her boy, and prayed a prayer of thanksgiving for his safe return.

FATE OF KEENAN AND PASCHAL FAMILIES, WINTER OF 1870.

Keenan's Branch, two and one-half miles southwest of Forrestburg, near the Little Berry White place, is a spot of historic interest to the pioneer settlers of Montague County. It was here the Keenan family lived, in their modest log cabin. Mrs. Paschal and her children made their home with them. With the thrift and economy characteristic of the pioneer they managed to provide the necessaries of life for the family. Mr. Keenan, after much deliberation as to the danger of making a trip in such troublous Indian times, decided to make a journey to Arkansas for apples to sell. He knew he could realize a good profit from his sales, as few, if any, apples were grown in Montague County at this time. Most unfortunately Mr. Keenan was blind, and because of this affliction he was always accompanied by one of his daughters. He prepared to make this journey in an ox wagon. He was not molested in any way, making the journey there and back in perfect safety; but upon his return, the first news he learned was the report of the terrible death of his wife and children. It happened in this way:

It was at the close of a winter's day. Mrs. Keenan had done the chores for the night, while Mrs. Paschal prepared the supper for the family. After partaking of their meagre meal the women and children gathered about the fireside, the children laughing and talking, as children will. Mrs. Keenan and Mrs. Paschal talked for some time of the work of spinning and weaving they had accomplished that day. Occasionally there was an anxious note in Mrs. Keenan's voice as she spoke of the possible dangers that might overtake her blind husband and daughter on their trip. Finally the children became sleepy and were tucked into bed, and Mrs. Paschal remarked that she was so tired she believed she would retire. But industrious Mrs. Keenan sat up knitting long after the others were sound asleep. She was possessed by a feeling of uneasiness. Her nervousness increased as she remembered that it was the time of the moon for the dreaded Indians to make their usual raids into the county. She listened intently—alert to every little noise—but she could hear nothing save the sound of an ox bell worn by oxen grazing on the grass near by, and the tinkle of the cow bells on her own cows in a lot close to the house. Finally even these noises ceased. The quiet stillness reassured her, and she, too, retired. Scarcely had she done so, and before she had time to go to sleep, the door, which was only fastened with a rope, was opened and an Indian thrust in his head. The noise aroused Mrs. Paschal and she began to scream loudly. The Indians, for there were more than one, beat her with a club and thrust a lance into her body, and otherwise mutilated her.

Mrs. Paschal and all of her children except two were killed outright. Mrs. Keenan was shot with an arrow before she could get out of bed. The Indians also scalped her. A baby and a little girl three years old were in bed with their mother, Mrs. Paschal. The girl was struck in the breast with a lance and left for dead. She afterwards recovered, but still carries the scar from the Indian's blow. She is now Mrs. Sweeten Williams of Denton Creek.

It is supposed that the Indians failed to see the baby, as it was left unharmed. In the excitement following the coming of the Indians little Ben Paschal slipped out of the door and ran down a string of fence, lying down in hiding until all the noise ceased, when he ventured to return to the house. Here he found a sight that would chill any heart. Poor, suffering Mrs. Keenan called him to her, and in tender tones advised him what to do. "Keep a close watch, my child, and if you see the Indians returning take your wounded little sister and the baby and crawl under the puncheon floor. No matter what happens, do not make a sound. Just let them finish killing me, then they will leave, and you will be spared."

The next morning she sent him to a neighbor's by the name of Ben Hodges, to tell him of their horrible plight. Before he got back a party of men passed that way and becoming suspicious of the general appearance of things proceeded to the house. They had found the ground covered with feathers. They suspected that it was the work of Indians, as it was their custom to rip open the beds and scatter the feathers in order to get the cloth.

Upon entering the house they found the dead bodies of the occupants lying about, and Mrs. Keenan in a half fainting condition. She was suffering intensely from her wounds. Mrs. Keenan and also the dead bodies were removed to the home of Mr. Roberts to be prepared for burial. However, Mrs. Keenan lived twelve days after she was scalped, suffering the most intense agony. Her constant prayer was that she might live to see her husband once more. But her prayer was not granted. She died before he returned.

Joe F. Box, Rufus Roberts, Bart and Wash Trailer rode all one day trying to get material with which to make Mrs. Keenan's coffin, but did not succeed in getting it. At last they were forced to carry planks, which were sixteen feet in length, from an old vacant house on the John Harviff place. They took the planks from the floor and carried them on horseback three and one-half miles, to the home of Mr Singletary, where the coffin was made. Mr. Singletary worked all night on the coffin, the men going back and forth for the lumber.

Mr. Joe Box, who was carrying a sixteen-foot plank, was riding a Spanish pony. It became frightened and ran away with him. In the darkness he became separated from his companions and it was with difficulty that he found them again. He was afraid to call them for fear of attracting the Indians. He finally reached Mr. Singletary's, still carrying the plank that he had started out with. The coffin was ready by the next morning and Mrs. Keenan was buried in the family graveyard near her home. The house in which Mrs. Keenan and the Paschals were attacked by the Indians was made of hewn logs, was about sixteen feet square, had only one door and one window. This window had no glass panes, but closed with a wooden shutter. Moccasin tracks were found near this window, and it was supposed that the Indians watched through the partly open board shutter until the women and children retired.

The Indians had a large drove of horses with them, and succeeded in making their way out of the county without being overtaken. There is little or nothing left to remind one of this sad tragedy. Today, if you should visit that portion of Montague County, you would find cultivated fields and homes of peace and plenty, where neighbors go to and fro without fear, and little children play in the sunshine and gather wild flowers in the woods with no thought of danger. Schools and churches are dotted here and there, for wherever the white man builds his home, evidences of culture and progress mark his footsteps.

EASTER SUNDAY, 1871.

A family by the name of Johnson lived on the McFarland place on Denton Creek. They had two sons, Will and Arch. Arch was a bright little fellow, very much liked in the neighborhood. One of the neighbors, Mr. Fred Broadstreet, who lived on Dry Valley, had made Arch a present of a pig. He had been wanting to go after it for some time, and persuaded his mother to allow him to go on Easter Sunday. His older brother, Will, was to accompany him, and their mother insisted that they return home early. She bade them good bye with many misgivings, for she was always in dread of the Indians.

They reached the Broadstreet home in safety, and soon started to return to their own home. Little Arch was carrying the pig in a sack. He was very proud of his possession, and as he trudged along by his brother's side his whole conversation was about the pig. They had not gone far until they were confronted by three mounted Indians, heavily armed. Will drew his gun, at the same time saying, "If you don't let me alone I will shoot you." He told Arch they would catch him if he didn't drop the pig. But from fear, or some unexplained reason, he still clung to the pig. One of the cruel, heartless Indians deliberately took aim at the little fellow, killing him instantly. They then turned and fled from the neighborhood without doing further harm to the settlement.

STORY OF BEALE AND MAXEY FAMILIES.

In the summer of 1872 several families were living together at John Stroud's for protection from the Indians. This was known as the "Stroud Settlement," and was about five miles southeast of Montague, at the head of Denton Creek. These families were living in camps and other shelters until they could build houses. Some of them had picket fences around their camps. The families living here were that of Jonathan Stroud, Tom Savage, Will Davis, Jet Davis, Jess Maxey, Joe Maxey and Mr. Beale.

Measles broke out in the company, and nearly all of the smaller children and some of the grown up people died from this disease, which was in a most violent form.

Jess Maxey had been freighting and as a consequence had not been at home in some time. When he returned to find the large number of deaths that had resulted from the epidemic of measles he became very much alarmed for fear his three children would be stricken with the dread disease. He and his father and the Beale family moved at once to the old Rice place, about one-half mile distant, hoping by this that their children would escape the malady. It meant, however, that they were only to meet a worse fate.

In a few days the Indians added another terrible deed to the history of their fiendish cruelties in Montague County, and the Beale and Maxey families were the victims. Mr. Beale and Mr. Maxey went to Montague on business, leaving Mr. Maxey's aged father as a protection for the women and children. Mr. Maxey, with his two grandchildren, a small boy and girl, and two of the Beale children were at the wood pile. The good old man was chopping wood while the children were playing together and gathering the chips. A band of Indians slipped up on them, taking them unawares. The women discovered the presence of the Indians first, and Mrs. Beale called frantically to them to come into the house. The little ones seeing the Indians became so badly frightened they ran to the corner of the fence and huddled up close together. They were immediately captured by the Indians. They killed the two Beale children on the spot with a gun, but their mother was not sure of it at this time. Mrs. Maxey was standing in the door with her baby in her arms, calling to the children, when an Indian fired at her. The shot struck the baby in the head, killing it instantly. The same bullet penetrated her arm. The women, when they saw they could not save their children, ran in and closed the front door. Mrs. Beale was slightly wounded by a bullet that was fired through the door. After this the women ran out the back door and on into the woods, where they remained in hiding until the return of their husbands, late that afternoon. The poor wounded mother carried the dead baby with her, and all day the two grief-stricken, terror-stricken women lay there, beset by a thousand fears.

When their husbands returned and they went back to the house, to add to their horror and grief, they found the poor old father lying dead in the yard and the two little Beale children, who had so lately been busy at play, all unconscious of danger, lying dead near the wood pile.

The two Maxey children had been captured and taken away, the bereaved parents being left to imagine their fate.

Three years had passed away and still the saddened parents had heard no news of their children, in spite of all their efforts to find some trace of them.

One day Mr. Bob Savage, one of our oldest settlers, who lives on Denton Creek, was in Montague and overheard some people talking about a little boy they had heard about in Fort Sill whom the Indians had stolen. The description of the child reminded Mr. Savage so much of Volley Maxey that he questioned the people closely. As he listened to their story he became more and more convinced that the child was Mr. Jess Maxey's son. He immediately went to the father and mother and told them about it. Their hopes ran high. The father at once began negotiations, through the government, and succeeded in getting back his long lost son. Imagine the joy of these parents at once more beholding their boy. (Many times has Mrs. Maxey been heard to say she could never express her gratitude toward Mr. Savage for being the means of the little son's being restored to her.) Mrs. Maxey never met Mr. Savage after this without shedding tears of joy. Long years have passed; the whole lives of Mr. Maxey and his wife have been saddened by the fate of their little daughter. She was a beautiful child, with winning manner. Volley said he never really knew what became of his little sister. She had been sick, and the journey soon tired her weakened little body. She was crying, and he said the Indians took her out in a thicket by the roadside, and he believed they killed her, as that was the last time he ever saw her. Where they threw her little body the wind sighs mournfully through the thicket; the birds she loved so well sing a refrain in the boughs near by, and the ground round about is carpeted with the flowers her little fingers had once delighted to gather.

CHARGING VICTORIA PEAK, SUMMER OF 1870.

On a calm summer day in 1870, about one hundred and fifty Indians charged the fort, at what is commonly known as Queen's Peak, against thirteen men. No one in the fort was hurt but a Dutchman, who was hiding up a chimney, was badly frightened. Two unknown men, who were with a party headed for Kansas with a herd of cattle, left the herd and started to the fort to ask some information. They rode right into the Indians, who had been storming the fort, and both men were slain. Some of the men from the fort were out with a herd of cattle, but fortunately they did not come in contact with the Indians. Two negroes on their way to the fort were killed on this same day by the Indians. The Indians called negroes buffalo soldiers, because of their color and because of their kinky hair. On this same day Boone Kilgore, a boy 12 years of age, was herding cattle alone, when he saw the Indians approaching. The Indians appreciated a good rider, and often a small boy owed his life to the fact that he was an expert horseman. They delighted to capture a boy who understood riding, because he would be useful to them in breaking wild horses. They would often take great pains to train a boy of this kind in all the Indian sports, and make him of service to them. As a rule they treated a captive of this kind fairly well.

Boone Kilgore was an expert horseman, which the Indians at once discovered, and they determined to capture him alive. Boone was riding a splendid horse, and being familiar with the crossings and trails the courageous little fellow would have made his escape, but the Indians circled around him and cut off his only hope of escape. They came nearer and nearer, and finally an Indian drew near enough to deal him a terrific blow on the head, knocking him off his horse. They captured him and the horse and went on their way. His father witnessed the whole scene from a distance and was so overcome with grief and rage it was with difficulty that his friends restrained him from following the band alone. Finally they convinced him that their small number would amount to nothing against such great odds. The Indians kept Boone for two or three months at Fort Sill. His father hearing of this went there, and with the help of the government bought his son back.

INDIAN MASQUERADES AS WOMAN.

It was customary in early days for the women to have what was called "the wash place." This was usually near some spring, as close to the house as possible. Some, not having washboards, laid their garments on a rude bench and "battled" them.

That is, they had a smooth paddle and beat them. When the washing process was finished the clothes were spread out on the bushes near by to dry. It was on a certain day in the winter of 1867 that a lone Indian, going by a woman's "wash place," saw the clothes drying on the bushes. A bright thought entered his cunning, treacherous brain. He would put on the woman's dress and bonnet and by that means he would be enabled to make his way through the country to the band from which he had strayed away, without harm to himself. Or, better still, it might permit him the fiendish pleasure of walking up on some unprotected woman and her children and killing them before they had time to suspect his identity. Filled with this thought, he sallied bravely forth, dressed in woman's garb. He had his bow and arrow with him, only half concealed by the folds of the dress he was wearing. He might have carried out his plans, but John McDaniel happened to be coming that way and caught a glimpse of his face, and saw the bow and arrow he was carrying. He quickly stepped back into the brush, unseen by the Indian. He waited until he passed by, then sprang out and clutched him from behind. Although hampered by the dress and taken by surprise the Indian fought desperately and a mighty struggle ensued. Mr. McDaniel was armed with a butcher knife, which the Indian, with all his strength, endeavored to pull through his hand, but the hardy frontierman's strength was more than a match for him and he finally slew the Indian with the butcher knife. He scalped him and tacked the scalp, together with the bow and quiver, on a board, and hung the board in his smoke house. Shortly after this a band of Indians passed that way, and it was always thought saw the scalp of this Indian. Such a sight always made them, if possible, more bloodthirsty than ever.

INDIANS ATTACK LEE HOME ON WHITE'S PRAIRIE.

In 1872 the Lee family was living on what was known as the "Old Pickett Ranch," on the borders of Montague and Jack Counties. The good old man was sitting just inside the door one day, reading his Bible. As he meditated upon the word of God, and of the great comfort he received from reading this sacred book, thoughts of Indian dangers faded from his mind. While he was thus engaged a band of Indians stealthily surrounded the house and left no way for escape. Their first act was to murder Mr. Lee, then killed and scalped his wife and one daughter. The Indians took the two smaller girls and one little boy away with them as captives. The children were afterwards bought back by friends and relatives.

On their way home from the reservation they stopped and spent the night with Mrs. Chesley Marlett, a pioneer mother of this county.

"SATANTA" AND "BIG TREE."

Satanta was a Kiowa Indian chief who was held in much dread by the white settlers. He is described as being of tall and commanding appearance; every inch the typical Indian warrior. In the various councils in which he sat Satanta's eloquence gained for him the sobriquet of "The Orator of the Plains." He was one of the original signers of the "Medicine Lodge Treaty" of 1867, by which his tribe consented to go on a reservation. Big Tree was another Kiowa Indian chief, who figured conspicuously in different raids made by the Indians upon the white people. In the spring of 1871 a large band of Indians, led by Chief Satanta, Chief Big Tree and Chief Satance attacked a government train en route from Jacksboro to Fort Griffin, in Shackleford County, to deliver flour to the United States troops stationed there. The expedition was in charge of Captain Julian Field of Mansfield, Tarrant County. This train of wagons was said to have been drawn by thirty-six strong mules. When within a few miles of where the town of Graham, in Young County, now stands the train was attacked by this band of Kiowa Indians. It is told that all of the drivers but two were slain and the wagons burned. The Indians took the mules with them to the reservation near Fort Sill. This incident, while it did not occur in Montague County, was near enough to strike terror to the hearts of the women and children, some of the men who were slain having friends in this county.

Not many hours before the attack recorded happened, General W. T. Sherman marched along the same route, on a tour of inspection of the forts along the frontier, and narrowly escaped coming in contact with this same band of Indians. He was accompanied as far as Red River by Mr. Bud Morris of Montague. When night came on Mr. Morris camped on this side of the river and General Sherman crossed over to the opposite bank. The river rose in the night, and as there was no ferry Mr. Morris had to abandon his trip to Fort Sill, General Sherman going on. General Sherman, in the meantime, had heard of the massacre of the government train. His indignation was aroused and he determined to make a thorough investigation, and sent General McKinzie to the scene of the killing to obtain the facts in the case. The frontier had not had sufficient protection from the Indians, and a number of Jacksboro citizens decided that this would be an opportune time to lay before the general the situation as it actually was. He was much impressed by what they told him. The result was when General Sherman arrived at Fort Sill he immediately began a search for the guilty parties. From the Indian agent he learned the names of the tribes who had participated in the killing of the teamsters. The Indians were overheard boasting of what they had done. As soon as he had sufficient proof of their guilt General Sherman ordered the arrest of Chief Big Tree, Chief Satance and Chief Satanta. A fight with these Indians was narrowly averted. When Satance was arrested he rushed toward one of the officers, flourishing a Bowie knife. Satance was instantly killed and Big Tree and Satanta were taken to Jacksboro for trial. They were tried, convicted and sentenced to be hanged, but their sentences were afterwards commuted to life imprisonment.

After these Indian chiefs had been taken to the penitentiary, to serve their terms, a treaty was entered into by the Government and the Indian tribes living on the Ft. Sill reservation. The Government of Texas also signed this treaty. The treaty provided that every Indian was to be placed on parole and must surely answer roll call every morning— and if they violated this parole they would immediately be taken as prisoners by the government authorities and carried to Florida. This treaty was the means of restoring confidence and courage along the entire frontier; as time went on the settlers found their confidence was not misplaced, for only a few raids occurred after this. After the treaty between the government and the Indian tribes, Governor Davis pardoned Chief Satanca and Chief Big Tree on condition that they return to their reservation and cease to molest the white people. This they readily agreed to do. It is said they had not been back on their reservation two weeks before old Chief Satanta went on the warpath again. He was arrested and sent back to the penitentiary at Huntsville. Mr. Bud Morris, of Montague, was visiting there and called on Satanta. Mr. Morris described him as being the most magnificent specimen of physical manhood he had ever seen. He talked with the chief for quite a while. Satanta asked him if he thought the authorities would ever let him out of prison again. Mr. Morris replied that he didn't think they ever would allow him his liberty again. Soon after this Satanta committed suicide by throwing himself from a balcony of the penitentiary. After all his wickedness it is sad to think how his wild, untrained nature must have longed intensely for the companionship of his people, for the freedom of the chase and for the pure air of the rolling prairies. Rather than be deprived of these pleasures he decided to journey to the "Happy Hunting Ground" of his Fathers. Big Tree, the Kiowa Indian chief, who was pardoned with Satanta, did not violate his parole. He was more easily subdued. Perhaps he was as anxious to wreak vengeance upon the white people as Chief Satanta, but thoughts of the rigid prison discipline to which he had been subjected and the dread of dreary confinement within the prison walls caused him to become submissive, outwardly at least, to the white man's law. Big Tree afterwards became a Christian, and has led a quiet peaceable life from that time on. In 1912 he was still living. His home was in Mountain View, Oklahoma. He is described as a very large man, who weighs nearly four hundred pounds.

THE INDIAN CROSSING—WHERE THE INDIANS CAME INTO, AND WENT OUT OF THE STATE.

Mr. and Mrs. John Hughes were among the first people who moved to this county. They came here in 1859, and settled at the "Head of Elm," where the town of St. Jo now stands. It was the year of the gold fever and the trail was thick with pack horses, and men, women and children—some on foot and some in wagons—all making a desperate effort to reach the gold region. Some said that gold was to be found in the Wichita Mountains, others said you would not find gold until you reached Pike's Peak. Mr. Hughes was among the many who were disappointed in their search for gold. He afterwards moved his family to Whitesboro. His daughter, Miss Regina Hughes, married Mr. Charles Moore in 1873, and they moved to the mouth of the Little Wichita River, in Clay County, just over the line from Montague County.

This was the point chosen by the Indians to come into the country on their raids, and to go out of the State on their return from harrassing the settlers by their savage depredations. For this reason they never molested the Moore family at any time; they could frequently hear the water splashing as the Indians were crossing the river. The last time they crossed over was in 1874, after the killing of the Huff family near Decatur, in Wise County. This marked their last entrance into Texas for warlike purposes. It was here that Jesse James, the notorious robber, spent the night with the Moore family. They did not know whom they had entertained until afterwards. Mrs. Moore had many exciting experiences with the Indians along the frontier in this and other counties. Mr. and Mrs. Moore now live in Forrestburg.

THE LAST INDIAN RAID IN MONTAGUE COUNTY.

On a certain day in August, 1872, a number of Montague County settlers engaged in a fight with the Indians. This proved to be the last Indian fight that occurred in this county.

A band of Indians had been raiding through the county, stealing horses as they went. Sometimes the Indians would remain in hiding during the day and would send out their spies, who, from some high point, or fringe of timber, would try to keep in touch with the movements of the white men of the settlement. This forced the settlers to be constantly on their guard in order to keep the Indians from committing depredations of all kinds. So many people were now coming into the county, thus reinforcing the protection of the settlement, that the Indians found it more difficult to operate their raids than in the past. But they were none the less ferocious and sought every opportunity to annoy the white settlers and to force them from what they were pleased to term "the land of their fathers."

On the day recorded, Levi Perryman, Aleck Perryman, Crede Roberts, Holloway Williams, Henry Williams, Henry Roberts, — Southward, — Southward's son, and some others whose names could not be learned, had two fights with the Indians. Mr. Levi Perryman had been elected that morning to command the company. The first fight occurred on Dry Valley, southeast of Montague, on what is now called the Jim Boyd place. Levi Perryman shot an Indian during this engagement, who afterwards died. The Indians became frightened and withdrew from the scene. The white men waited a few minutes for Bob Bean and his company. They failed to appear and the men left in pursuit of the Indians. They overtook them three miles west of Cash McDonald's and exchanged a few shots. Mr. Perryman ordered the men to retreat and fall back with the company of white men that he thought was coming behind. They failed, however, to meet the other company. The Indians were advancing so fast, Mr. Perryman saw they would soon overtake them, and he ordered his men to dismount and get ready for battle. This they refused to do, and the men, using their own judgment, separated, going in different directions. Just before this Holloway Williams had remarked that he ought to go back, as he was riding a tired horse, but said if Levi would stay with him he would go on. Mr. Perryman promised, for he knew Williams was a good fighter. The Indians were now gaining on them every minute. After the men refused to dismount Mr. Perryman told Williams to "bear to the left," through some thicket timber. Mr. Perryman lingered, to hold the Indians back until Mr. Williams could have time to get ahead, then he was going to catch up with him and take him up behind him, as he always rode a fine horse that was well able to carry two people. While he waited, an Indian ran up on him. As he was getting ready to shoot two more Indians appeared. Fearing they would overpower him he put spurs to his horse to overtake Williams (and incidentally, perhaps, with some view of getting away from the Indians). When overtaken Williams was urging his horse along as best he could. Levi said, "Stop beating your horse. There are only three Indians behind us, and we can whip them without any trouble, and you can get behind me on my horse if more Indians come and we will get away in a hurry." No Indians appeared, but "whang" came a bullet over the hill.

Levi said, "I'm going, I'm afraid some of the boys are in trouble." About this time the Indians shot at Mr. Perryman. Williams said, "Why do you wait? Go on and leave me, and try to save yourself." This Mr. Perryman refused to do. Appreciating the constancy of his friendship, Williams said, "Levi, you are worth a thousand dollars in gold to me." In a few minutes the two men were joined by Alec Perryman.

As no further signs of the Indians were given the three men decided to go to the McFarland home, some distance away. There they found Crede Roberts, who told them about an Indian he had killed. The men had intended to go on until they met Bob Bean's company, but after they met Crede Roberts they decided to go with him and find the Indian he had slain. They asked Crede how it happened, and he told the following story:

When the men separated, as has already been told, Crede Roberts, some way, got behind the others.

The Indians, eighteen in number, were hid in the black jack flat and charged on the white men. They failed to shoot any of the men, but wounded Crede Roberts' horse in the leg. He soon discovered that his horse could not carry him further, and he slided off the horse into the tall grass. He struck the horse and he ran on a little further. The Indians followed, thinking he was still riding it. When they came upon the wounded horse and found him without a rider they knew at once that the man had employed strategy to deceive them. They halted for a minute and decided to hunt for Crede. In and out, in and out, of the tall grass they rode, searching for him. A number of Indians passed right by where he lay in hiding but failed to notice him. The last one to come behind all the other Indians was their chief. Mr. Roberts at once recognized the horse he was riding as one the Indians had stolen from Mr. Leeper. With keen, trained eye and haughty mien he looked among the tall grasses, hoping to detect some sign that would lead him to discover the hidden man. The white man saw him, but feared to fire because he knew the report would attract the other Indians to the spot, when he would doubtless be killed. But he was forced to fire in self-defense. Just as he thought he was going to pass on by without seeing him, the chief glanced down and saw him lying in the tall grass almost at his horse's feet. For a second they looked into each other's eyes and the chief drew his gun to fire, but Roberts was too quick for him. He fired first, killing him instantly. The shot attracted the other Indians and they began to assemble for battle. Great confusion reigned when they found their chief had been slain. Mr. Roberts said he had never heard such moaning as the Indians did. They circled around their dead chief, chanting the weird monotonous chant of their tribes.

In the excitement following this Mr. Roberts managed to make his escape unnoticed. Walking was too slow a means of travel that morning, and he said he ran several miles without stopping until he reached the McFarland place on Denton Creek. In the race he lost his hat and gun, but afterwards recovered both. When he had finished his story Levi Perryman said, "Crede, if I had known your horse was wounded and you left behind on foot I would have stayed with you if I had known the Indians would have killed me."

By this time they had reached the spot where the killing took place and found the dead chief lying where he fell. His warriors had spread two calico shirts and a blanket over his body. The Indians had also left the horse he was riding, tied near by. This was the first time they had ever been known to leave one behind, but according to their ancient superstitious Indian custom they left him there for the chief to ride home to the "happy hunting ground of his fathers." But instead of their chief riding him, as they in their ignorance believed he would, the men took the horse back to its rightful owner. The State of Texas gave Crede Roberts a $50 rifle as a reward for killing the Indian, and the neighbors made up money and bought him another horse.

The killing of this Indian took place southwest of Salona, between Sunset and Salona. The minute men had previously been notified to head the Indians off at Brushy Mound. These men were commanded by Capt. J. J. Willingham. The men remained on duty until sundown, when a man named Harmon was sent to notify them that the Indians had fled, bound for the Indian Territory.

The story of this Indian raid is of much interest to the old settlers, for it marked the dawn of a new era in Montague County. For, in 1872, the faithful runner, who risked his life many times over to warn the settlers of the incoming Indian bands, made his last ride on this errand of mercy. It was never necessary again. The words that had struck terror to the hearts of the women and children, "Get up your horses, get ready your firearms, for the Indians are on the way, killing and burning as they come," these words were to be heard in this county no more. The death knell of the Indian raids was sounded and Montague County knew her red foe never again.

About this time the State began to increase its

ranger forces and stationed them along the frontier in such an effective way that they made Indian invasion almost impossible. This brought about a feeling of security that had not heretofore been enjoyed by the settlers, and the county entered upon an era of progress and prosperity.

JIM NED LOOKOUT.

Jim Ned Lookout is an object of much interest to the people of this county. It was here, in the early days of the settlements, that the wary Indian spy would climb to the top of "Jim Ned Lookout" to survey the country and thereby ascertain the movements of the unsuspecting white people. Jim Ned Lookout is a mound or high prairie ridge that took its name from Jim Ned, a Caddo Indian chief. This chief had but one eye. By climbing to the highest point on this mound he could see, with the keen, trained eye of the eagle, for miles around. To the spy system employed by the Indians was due many of the successful attacks made upon the early settlers. Jim Ned died in Kansas in 1863, on the Virdigris River. His death resulted from smallpox. No trappings of the warrior were buried with him, that he might make a brave appearance when he arrived at the "happy hunting ground" of his imagination. He was wrapped in a blanket and buried in a shallow grave near the banks of the Virdigris. Jim Ned Lookout is between Montague and Forrestburg. The Dye Mound road leads around the north side of it and the Forrestburg and Montague road leads by the south side of the Mound. Solemn and solitary it stands in the winter's cold and the balmy springtime, holding the secrets of the long ago, when the haughty Indian chiefs assembled in council to declare eternal warfare against the "pale faces," who were striving to wrest from them the land of their fathers. They viewed, with increasing hatred, their encroachment upon their hunting grounds, and vowed a vow to "spare not." But in this land which the Indian apparently thought was created for him, his descendants are no more. Further and further away he has been driven until at the present he is little more than a tattered remnant upon the fringe of the civilization his savage nature deplores.

BRUSHY MOUND.

They tell us that the scenery of Colorado bankrupts the English language; that the glory of the Yosemite Valley has passed into literature; that the grandeur of the Rocky Mountains has been told in song and story. And this is true. But when all has been said we will find that nature has not been unkind to Montague County, but has rather been disposed to distribute her gifts with a generous hand.

Streams flow through the boundaries of our county upon whose banks grow the spreading shade trees. Pecan orchards are to be found growing without cultivation and producing an abundant yield. The wild grape vine sways gracefully from the boughs of the trees that have given it friendly support, and there are to be found many charming spots where picnic parties may spend the day most pleasantly, while they breathe in the pure, balmy life-giving breezes peculiar to this climate. If we cannot go through the Grand canyon of the Colorado, climb Pike's Peak, visit Niagara Falls, tour California and pitch pebbles into the Pacific Ocean, let's not be disappointed. We can have a good time at home. Let us pack our baskets with a nice lunch, invite a few congenial friends and go "picnicing" in our own neighborhood. We cannot drive five miles in any direction on a clear spring morning in Montague County without finding a pleasant place to spend the day. You will find pretty flowers, inviting shades and blue skies. Let us not find fault with home, but let us cultivate a spirit of appreciation for our own surroundings.

One of the most picturesque places in the County is "Brushy Mound." It is five miles from Bowie, and is a part of the ranch owned by Mr. Z. T. Lowrie of Bowie. The accessibility of Brushy Mound and the comparative ease with which it may be explored adds greatly to the pleasure of a visit to this place. It is made cool and inviting by the growth of shade trees which cling to the soil that has gathered among the rocks. The curious rock formations are of interest, even to the accustomed eye. Truly these formations are wonderful, as wonderful as the presence of the Mound itself. Rising abruptly from a stretch of prairie, it gives a commanding view of the surrounding country. In the distance to the right is to be seen another mound. This point is called Queen's Peak.

Doubtless these mounds are centuries old, and for ages they have stood, like two silent sentinels, guarding the stronghold of their people. Queen's Peak took its name from a young girl whose name was Queen Victoria. She was stolen by the Indians, who, in their flight, crossed the extreme top of the mound. A piece of the girl's dress was afterwards found here and the people christened the spot Queen's Peak. Brushy Mound has ever been a favorite retreat for picnic parties. One spot full of interest to the visitor is a large, smooth rock. This rock is almost covered by the names and dates carved on it by the merry parties that have gathered there from year to year.

Brushy Mound is not without its historic interest. It was from its heights the wary Indian viewed the surrounding country and lay in wait for the early settlers. On the very top is an Indian grave. How long it has been here we do not know. But some time in the long ago the Indians assembled here to practice their weird incantations over the grave of this warrior.

How old are these rocks? No man knows. But as one gazes upon this great rugged mass they cannot but wonder if this upheaval came on that memorable day when the "Man of Galilee" bore His cross up Calvary's hill and the "rocks and the mountains were rent in twain."

THE HOME OF MY EARLY DAYS.

There is an old cabin at the foot of the hill,
    And my heart turns to it today;
The lord of his manor may jeer if he will,
    But I will continue my lay,
And will sing of the cabin both old and uncouth,
    The unsightly old cabin, the home of my youth.

Around the old cabin the wild flowers grew,
    And I gathered them there in my play;
They sparkled like diamonds, in the fresh morning dew,
    As I bore them triumphant away—
To the door of our cabin at the foot of the hill—
    The rugged old cabin, low perched by the rill.

And mother would chide me for running away,
   To a place where an Indian might be;
And tell me the evils in my pathway that lay,
   If my wanderings the savage might see;
But greater the pleasure compared to the fear,
   Was there in the cabin on the Texas frontier.

Though few were the comforts, as judging by now,
   What the people desire and possess;
A feeling of bliss there existed somehow,
   And a longing to cherish and bless;
No selfishness reigned, as sometimes we find
   In the homes of today more gay and refined.

The stranger was welcome to such as we had;
   A neighbor was precious as gold;
We saw his good traits instead of his bad,
   In the beautiful seasons of old,
In the old-fashioned cabin, so modest and plain,
   And that is the life I long for again.
                  —By L. Passmore.

THE HOME LIFE OF THE PIONEER.

A clearing in the woods, with a rail or picket fence surrounding it. A well beaten path that led to the spring and wash place near by. One large log room, with sometimes a side room, with a square opening cut for a window. This window had no glass panes, but a wooden shutter, held in place by leather straps, served as a closing. Two doors, one in front, the other at the back; a puncheon or dirt floor and a stick and clay chimney. A large fireplace opened inside the house. Across this fireplace was a goodly sized iron bar on which the pot hooks hung. Unlike her daughters and granddaughters, who cook on a modern range heated by wood, coal or gas, the pioneer mother prepared her meals and cooked them on the fireplace. Many an appetizing meal was served to the family in this way. Another essential was the large iron oven. It stood on tall iron legs, and was covered with a heavy iron lid. When baking, this oven was set over a bed of red hot coals, and coals were heaped on top of the lid. This was the favorite way of baking bread. A well worn stone step at the front door, some rude boxes nailed on the outside on either side of the door, in which bloomed the old-fashioned moss. There were beds of zenias, marigolds, bachelor buttons and princess feather, grown from seed brought from the old states; a rude bench under a shade tree, the grind stone near by, the ash hopper in the back yard and almost invariably a horse hitched at the front gate.

Get this description in your mind and you will have a picture of the pioneer home of Montague County. The home life in any pioneer country is much the same. There is very little difference in their environment. The people, in many instances, being taxed to the uttermost to provide the necessaries of life. Luxuries were unthought of. The markets were far away and the price of sugar and coffee was so high that no doubt many of our good pioneer mothers could instruct us in the art of using cane syrup for sugar and parched grain for coffee.

Too much cannot be said in praise of the resourcefulness of the housewife of early Montague County days. She had none of the modern appliances for lightening labor, such as we now have in daily use. Most of the labor was performed with her own willing hands. Corn meal constituted the principal bread making. Flour being scarce biscuits were only served on rare occasions, many families being without any flour whatever. An old price list was consulted and it was found that during this period white sugar was 35 cents per pound; rice, 25 cents per pound; hams, 35 cents per pound; brown sugar, 20 cents per pound; corn, $1.37 per bushel; barley, $2 per bushel; oats, $1.50 per bushel, and flour, $15 per barrel of 196 pounds. Salt, 5 cents per pound, and beef cattle, $35 per head. Almanacs could be had for 25 cents each, by going to Gainesville for them. It was not uncommon for people to get without bread stuff and remain without for days. Mr. Bud Morris of Montague said he went to mill twice a year, in the spring and in the fall. He had to take his wheat to Dallas to have it ground into flour.

Corn was ground into meal by hand, in an old steel mill made for that purpose. The early settlers of Montague County shared the same experience.

The story is told of a family by the name of Penton, who, in 1866, lived near where Burlington now stands. They had to go forty-five miles to mill. Once when the father had been absent for a long time, looking after cattle, the family was without bread for three weeks. They had been living on sweet potatoes, dried beef and coffee made from wheat. As this supply was running low, the mother finally decided to send her two sons, Price, aged 9 years, and John, aged 13 years, to mill. The little fellows bade their mother good bye and, with scant rations on which to make the trip, they started for the mill, forty-five miles away.

They were driving a yoke of young steers and had eight bushels of corn with them which they expected to have ground into meal. The country was infested with Indians, and it was with many fears for their safety that the mother watched them start on their journey. She did not allow them to carry arms. She reasoned with them in this way: "If the Indians overtake you, and you make an attempt to fight them, they will kill and scalp you. Otherwise they may only take you captives, and you may have an opportunity to escape."

On their way they had to pass directly by the place where the Box family was attacked by the Indians and Mr. Box was slain. If their hearts beat more quickly and they urged the steers to travel faster at this point, who can blame them? They were five days making the trip. At night they would hobble the steers, put bells on them and turn them loose to graze on the grass. After eating a meal of dried beef and sweet potatoes the two boys would make their bed under the wagon and sleep there until morning. They made the journey there and back in safety. The mother spent many anxious hours watching for their return. Her joy was great when late one afternoon she saw the wagon slowly approaching, with both boys waving to her. Together with the smaller children she went down the road to welcome them back home. The family enjoyed the first bread they had tasted in weeks that night for supper.

Some one may ask, how could a mother send two young boys on such a perilous trip? Necessity knows no law, and it was necessary for them to go in order that the family might not suffer want. This is only an example of the many sacrifices and hardships the pioneer mothers were called upon to endure. In those troublous Indian times no wife or mother, when she said farewell to husband or children for only a brief period, had the assurance that she would ever see them again. Those were days of economy, too. They even had to economize in matches. Nowadays we think nothing of using a box of matches every few days, especially if we burn gas. Matches were not so common as they are today. The careful housewife kept the coals in the fireplace covered with ashes, that she might not be without the means of lighting a fire. Sometimes the fire would go out in spite of all precaution, and then they had to resort to the flint from the gunlock, using cotton to catch the spark with. Nothing was farther from our gas and electric lights of today than the tallow candles in early use. They were manufactured at home, and poured into moulds made especially for that purpose. Many people used a yarn strip dipped in grease and hung in some kind of a tin can for a light. Later these were supplanted by the small brass lamp without any chimney. It was surprising how soon a lamp of this kind could smoke the walls of a room. The task of providing clothing for the family also devolved upon the pioneer housewife. A great deal of her time was spent in spinning and weaving cloth from which the wearing apparel for the entire family was made. The wool garments were woven from wool clipped from the sheep. Cotton garments were woven from cotton which had previously been picked from the seed by hand. This was a most tedious process. They had certain ways of dyeing the cloth, and some very pretty homespun dresses were made. In those days clothes were made with a view to long wearing. You would think the costumes worn by many of the pioneer men quite odd looking. Borrowing some ideas from the Indians they quite often dressed in trousers made of buckskin, and a coonskin cap, with the tail left dangling from the back of the cap. The men also wore shawls and blankets. Immediately following reconstruction days it suddenly became necessary for two well reared, well educated and (before the war) wealthy gentlemen from the old states to make a quick journey to Texas. A friend of theirs, who had perhaps been a little too active in the Klu Klux Klan, had preceded them some months before. These men went to where their friend lived, and were directed to a spot where he was found trying to smoke a rabbit out of a log for supper. Upon seeing their friend, whom they had always seen attired in the prevailing fashion, dressed in the frontiersman garb of buckskin trousers, fawn skin vest and coon skin cap, they laughed until the tears ran down their cheeks. But a few weeks found them wearing the same kind of a costume, and taking upon themselves the habits of the new country— meeting its hardships and privations without a murmur.

There were few, if any, orchards in the early Montague County days, but here the thrifty housewife again met the emergency by drawing upon the wild fruit native to this county. They made palatable preserves from the wild plum and wild grape, not to mention the beer made from the persimmon.

It was the pride of the ambitious housewife to

have a large supply of feather beds and feather pillows. With all of the modern sanitary mattresses nothing makes a more comfortable bed upon which to rest the tired body than a well sunned, well aired feather bed. The women also helped in the making of ammunition, which was scarce in those days. The bullets were made from bars of lead bought at the hardware store. This was melted and poured into bullet moulds made for that purpose. They opened and closed like a pair of scissors. Their starch was made at home from potatoes. Every household made their own soap, and no back yard was complete without an ash hopper. A great deal of the furniture was made by the father out of timber brought from the woods. Some people only had a footboard and one side to their bed. This was nailed up in one corner of the room, the headboard and one side consisting of the sides of the house. Tables and benches were also made at home from the timbers of the forest, while chairs were fashioned from the same material, the bottoms being made of rope or rawhide.

It was a long time before sewing machines came into general use, the women doing their sewing by hand. They had few clocks, the time of day being reckoned by the sun. The pioneer woman seldom spent an idle moment, so much depended upon her. Not only was she expected to care for the house, prepare meals, wash, iron, sew and look after the children, but she had to manufacture so much that was used for home consumption.

Some of the old leather covered, weather-beaten trunks in the far corner of some of these log cabins on the frontier, when opened would tell of a far different life to this that was led in the old states. Lift the lid, and in the bottom, carefully wrapped, you will find one or two silk dresses, some dainty linen and lace, kid gloves and a pair of satin slippers. A tinge of sadness comes into the mother's face as she allows her thoughts to wander for a moment to the days of long ago, but she bravely puts such thoughts away and takes up her daily task again without complaint. The settlements were not without some social recreation. Open-hearted hospitality prevailed. The young people frequently gave dances, play parties and candy breakings. A house raising was looked forward to with much eagerness, this being the time for great exhibitions of strength. But the pleasure of all pleasure, that outshone them all, that was talked about for weeks before and for days afterward, was the good old-fashioned quilting, where the friends were invited, the quilt quilted and a sumptuous dinner was served. Those days had much of pleasure in them, for all they were mingled with anxieties, discomforts and inconveniences. This has given way to the path of progress, except the imprint of the character of the men and women of those times. These are stamped indelibly upon their children today—to overcome obstacles, to do things worth while, was their motto. Let that motto be yours.

TO THE BOYS AND GIRLS.

There is scarcely a boy or girl in our county who has not at some time been an interested listener to the stories told by the family fireside of what grandfather and grandmother had to tell of "Indian times." How they bravely defended their little cabin homes from the dreaded foe; how grandmother helped by the use of her rifle. A manly little hand rests lovingly on her shoulder, and a pair of inquisitive, bright eyes look into hers; her favorite grandson looks at the kind, wrinkled face and at the hands that have never known aught but kindly deeds, and says: "I just can't imagine grandmother firing a gun, but I know she has, 'cause she says so." Then the little fellow straightens himself up and, with all the ardor of the American boy, says: "I just wish I could have lived in those days. I would have helped you fight the Indians, grandfather." The old man's eyes kindle with the fires of youth as he replies: "I know you would, son. That is the kind of spirit Texas produces. Your father did before you. But the Indian times are no more. Father and grandfather settled with them."

But there is always a battle to be fought for right against the wrong. I want you to make a good soldier in that battle. The pioneers of this county laid the foundation for a worthy citizenship, and all we ask our sons and daughters is to be true to that principle. Be loyal, be honest, be honorable, be patriotic. Upon a patriotic citizenship depends the life of a nation. Study with your teacher the many meanings of the word patriotism. It does not always mean to take up weapons and go to war. It is the desire which aims to serve one's country, either in defending it from invasion or protecting its rights, and maintaining its laws and institutions in vigor and purity. You boys and girls belong to the twentieth century. Wonderful progress awaits you in the future. You may fly to Galveston in an air ship or live to see a gold mine in Montague County, but do not let your eager hopes of the future lessen your interest in the past.

Go to some old pioneer in your neighborhood; he may be feeble, but he can tell you many interesting experiences of the early days of your county. His memory carries him far back before we had the telegraph and the telephone, or the railroads. He can tell you when there was not a town in the county, and when they had no regular roads to travel; of when sugar was scarce and ice an undreamed of luxury. When it is your privilege to meet one of the old settlers of this county give them a cordial greeting and tell them how much you appreciate what they have done for our county. In a few years more all the pioneers who can tell you of the early days will be gone. Cultivate for them a feeling of patriotic reverence, for they are in every way worthy of it.

"I'LL DO WHAT I CAN."

Who takes for his motto, "I'll do what I can,"
   Shall better the world as he goes down life's hill,
The willing young heart makes the capable man,
   And who does what he can oft can do what he will.
There's strength in the impulse to help things along,
   And forces undreamed of will come to the aid
Of the one who, though weak, yet believes he is strong,
   And offers himself to the task unafraid—

I'll do what I can, is a challenge to fate,
   And fate must succumb when it's put to the test,
A heart that is willing to labor and wait
   In its tussle with life ever comes out the best.
It puts the blue imps of depression to rout,
   And makes many difficult problems seem plain;
It mounts over obstacles, dissipates doubt,
   And unravels kinks in life's curious chain.

I'll do what I can keeps the progress machine
  In good working order as centuries roll;
And civilization would perish, I do ween,
  Were those words not written on many a soul.
They fell the great forests, they furrow the soil,
  They seek new inventions to benefit man,
They fear no exertion, make pastime of toil,
  O, great is earth's debt to "I'll do what I can."
              —By Ella Wheeler Wilcox.

ODE TO MONTAGUE COUNTY.

"Oh, old Montague, when I gaze upon thy rugged
    face,
And on thy curious rocks
The hand of nature trace,
The straight and mighty clefts,
With which thy hills are riven,
As though some mighty hand
His sword had through them driven,
I wonder at the cause of thy mysterious birth,
What hand could dress thy adamantine rocks,
Or ope at will thy myriad pebbled locks.
Naught but the tossing of the mighty sea
Could thus unite them for Eternity—
'Tis said that in the eons of some ages past,
Old Ocean held this land within its grasp,
That rock and shell and bones of fish all tell

How from his sway the mighty monarch fell,
Gave back to life this sunny land of ours,
Where man and bird have built their sweetest bow-
 ers,
Where herds of cattle graze, and sweetest flowers
 blow,
Where farmers reap the golden headed mow,
Where many fruits their beauteous wealth unfold,
And forth are sent to countless homes untold—
And yet thy rolling plains and wooded hills,
Thy fields of cotton ripening for the mills,
Thy wealth of fruit, grape, berry,
Wherein the golden harvest all are merry,
Are naught to treasures rich within thy bosom sealed,
For thy deep mysteries are only half revealed.
In nature's reservoir these treasures lie concealed,
Montague, thy future sons, rich heritage shall reap,
From 'neath the soil in which their fathers sleep.
Shall we not love this happy land most blest,
Shall we not bleed to see its wrongs redressed,
Shall not its mothers rear their sons for noble deed,
Its men be brave, for right the first to lead,
Shall we not emulate the great of ancient story,
And be Montague our greatest pride and glory?"

—Mrs. Jennie Linnen.

MONTAGUE COUNTY.

Situated in North Texas, bordering the Red River, is an area of 976 square miles. This portion of country is known as Montague County, and is bordered on the south by Jack and Wise counties. Wise County is in North Texas. This county was organized in 1858, named for Henry A. Wise. Wise County has an area of 843 square miles. Decatur is the county seat. Jack County was organized in 1857. Has an area of 858 square miles. Was named for Patrick A. Jack. Jacksboro is the county seat. Montague County is bordered by Cook County on the east and by Clay County on the west. Cook County is situated in North Texas on Red River, was organized in 1849. Has an area of 1000 square miles. Was named for William G. Cook. The county seat is Gainesville. Clay County is in North Texas, bordering Red River. This county was organized in 1873. Was named for Henry Clay. Has an area of 1250 square miles. Henrietta is the county seat. Montague County was created by act of the Legislature in 1857. The county was organized the first Monday in August, 1858, and was named for Colonel Daniel Montague. He was district surveyor when the county was created. The home of Colonel Montague was four miles northwest of Gainesville. Colonel Montague's duties as surveyor frequently brought him in contact with the people of this county, and as a mark of esteem, when the county was created they gave it his name. Wise, Montague, Clay and Jack counties were created from Cook County. Cook County was created from Fannin County. The population of Montague County had now grown to sufficient number to justify local self-government. A general desire for civil measures for the protection of personal and property rights was now being manifested. Previous to this Montague County had been attached to Cook County for judicial purposes, but Gainesville was too far away for the convenience of the people. Accordingly an election was held for the purpose of selecting a suitable place for the county seat and for the election of county officers. At this election sixty-three votes were polled. Three places were candidates for the county seat. One place was known as the Head of Elm, where St. Jo now stands. Another was a place on Farmers' Creek, between Montague and Elm, owned by a man named Thomas. This man was the first Adjutant General Texas ever had. He owned a section of land there and proposed to give the county half of it if they would locate the county seat at this place, but the majority voted for the center of the county, which was afterwards named Montague. The county seat was founded in 1858. No one lived here at this time, and nothing about the place indicated that it would ever be a town. The sole tenants consisted of a solemn looking group of postoak trees.

A town lot sale soon followed, the lots ranging in price from $60 to $100. A log court house was built and used until after the war. Later an old store building that stood on the north side of the square was used for the court house. After this the frame court house burned, losing surveyor's records and other valuable papers. In 1878 a contract was let for a stone court house. This building was completed in 1879. Burned in 1884. All papers that were outside the vaults were destroyed. It was after this second disaster that the present court house was built. This building was so badly damaged by a severe wind storm in the spring of 1912 that a new court house became necessary. This new building will doubtless be erected soon, and it is to be hoped will be a credit to a county like Montague.

The result of the first election held in this county, so far as can be obtained is as follows:

County Judge—Dr. N. H. O. Polly.
Sheriff—Willis Lavender.
County Clerk—M. M. Hagler.
County Treasurer—Isaac Burnett.
County Commissioners—Austin Morris, — Edwards, E. S. Singletary.
County Surveyor—F. M. Totty.

The county's legal business was transacted in quite a different manner to what it is now. The Collector's and Assessor's office was one office and looked after by one man. The county had no County Attorney, such as we have now. The duties of this office were looked after by the District Attorney. This was changed in accordance with the Constitution in 1876. The first assessment of taxes was in 1859. The same man assessed and collected. He assessed one year and collected the next. That is, taxes assessed in 1859 would be collected in 1860. The assessor had to hunt up the taxpayer. The county was so thinly settled at this period one man could do the work in two weeks. The officers were not compelled to live in the county seat. The County Treasurer lived near Hardy (as did also the County Judge). The County Treasurer would put the county's money in his saddle bags, ride over to Montague, pay the officers their meager salaries and return home.

Contrary to present custom, an official term consisted of four years.

Officeholders in the early days of Montague County could not be accused of desiring office for mercenary purposes. For holding office then was an empty honor. They received little or no pay for their services, which they gave cheerfully, in order that a foundation for the executive department of the county might be laid. In 1858 there were only two voting precincts in the county, one located west of Forrestburg, where Levi Perryman now lives, the other was located at the Head of Elm, where St. Jo now stands. Some noted pioneer lawyers of the county were Colonel Maines, John Scanlin, Mr. Jamison, Mr. Matlock, John H. Stephens, W. H. Grigsby, Mr. Willis and J. M. Chambers. Some famous cases that have been tried at different times in the early court days of the county were the Cribbs and Preston case and the Brown case. Another noted case was that of Harris. According to his own confession, Harris, who lived alone with his brother, told his brother he was going away to seek work. He slipped back next morning and shot his brother while he was preparing his breakfast. His purpose was to get possession of his brother's property. He was tried and sentenced to be hanged. This was the only legal hanging which ever occurred in this county, although a large number of hangings in which the law was not invited to take part happened at other times. At this period the people were in constant danger of having their horses stolen by the Indians, who would come sometimes two hundred in a bunch and go as far as Denton town, then sweep back across this county with a thousand horses at a time. The Indians were raiding through the county at all times, but occasionally the people suffered a loss of horses at the hands of white people.

One hanging long remembered by old settlers was that of Nancy Hill, a notorious horse thief of that day. The hanging took place in 1873 on Denton Creek, about one hundred yards from the iron bridge on the Montague and Bowie road. The body was found hanging from the limb of a tree by Bud Morris of Montague. The woman had been followed from Springtown by a band of men, where she had been appropriating other people's horses. They came up on her at Denton Creek, and taking the law in their own hands meted out punishment by hanging. Another case particularly remembered by early settlers is that of the first man ever indicted in the county. He was indicted for stealing horses. His name was Jones and he operated his business under the guise of a preacher. He was very pious and benign in appearance, and it was a great shock to the county when he was arrested for stealing a horse from a man named Kelly. By his own statement he was 77 years old, and had followed horse stealing all his life. He had a novel way of hiding the horses' tracks. He put sheepskin moccasins on their feet and in that way avoided detection. He was tried and sentenced to twelve years in the penitentiary.

The first postoffice in the county was established at Montague in 1858. The mail carrier brought the mail twice a week from Gainesville. This seemed a long step toward progress to Montague County citizens, for previous to this they had to go to Decatur or Gainesville to get their mail.

Cattle raising was the principal pursuit in that day. In 1872 the office of Hide and Animal Inspector was created. J. T. Bellows was one of the first men who held this office. This office became necessary because of the large herds of cattle that were constantly being driven over the old Chism trail on the way to Kansas. This trail crossed Red River at Red River Station, in this county. In such large herds there was danger of other people's cattle straying into the herds. To assist in restoring such cattle to their rightful owners the law required these cattlemen to have what was termed a road brand. The Hide and Animal Inspector was stationed at Red River and all cattle failing to be branded with the "road brand" were driven out of the herd and either returned to the owner or sold and the money returned to the owner. Sometimes the officer would receive letters from individuals two hundred miles away describing their cattle. This office was discontinued about 1882. Railroad building relieved the necessity for trail driving as the cattle could now be shipped by rail.

One of the great incentives to immigration to an unsettled country is the liberal land grants offered by the government. When the settlers first came to Montague County there was no pre-emption law. Prior to January, 1836, any citizen could take up claims and settle anywhere they pleased. They held what was termed a "headright certificate," which entitled them to 4,060 45-100 acres of land. This law was in force for quite a while. In 1859 the pre-emptors had to live on their claims three years and pay 50 cents an acre for same.

In 1870 the Legislature created an act giving one hundred and sixty acres of land to heads of families and eighty acres to young men without families.

This act also forced them to live on the land three years, erect a house and at the end of that time survey the lines and make application for a patent right, when he became the legal owner of the land.

It was but natural that many would be found who were courageous enough to try their fortunes in this frontier country.

There is something wonderfully inspiring about a new country. And notwithstanding the frontier settlements suffered heavily from Indian depredations, there was not found wanting those who turned their steps toward Montague County with hopeful faces. As a first view of this new country burst upon their vision they were pleased with the prospect. The stretches of prairie were green with vegetation and brilliant with wild flowers, while groups of timber were dotted here and there. The soft winds wafted sweetest perfume to the delighted beholder, who, as he surveyed the splendid view let thoughts of the dreaded Indian fade from his mind for the moment.

The growth and subsequent development of Montague County may be traced to a single imperishable feature—"Determination." The pioneer men and women, who have seen the county emerge from savagery to civilization, possessed this characteristic to a marked degree. It takes courage and determination to face the situation as it existed in Montague County at that time. Neighbors were few and far between; there were no schools, no churches, no telephones, no telegraph, no railroads, no gas, no electric lights, no well built, well furnished homes, no postoffice in the county, no buggies, no carriages, no cooking stoves, no automobiles, no pianos, no organs; as one pioneer expressed it—no nothing— but a country inhabited by warlike tribes of Indians. But there was something in the very nature of the early settlers that helped them to overcome difficulties and brought civilization, with all of its attendant comforts, to their door.

The county, despite the dangerous times, was not without a halo of romance. Many a young bride went to housekeeping as happy in her modest log cabin and crude surroundings as a princess in a palace. The first marriage in the county was that of Sam Spray and Miss Bradin.

A marriage around which much interest centered was that of W. B. Savage and Miss Liza Ann Taylor in 1857. This was the first wedding to occur on Denton Creek. This estimable couple have lived in Montague County ever since. They have known the county in its stormiest days and in its periods of peace and prosperity. It is a pleasure to visit in their good home. During this period there was no such institution as a public school. If there had been the people would have been too keenly alive to the danger of their children being killed or captured by the Indians to have allowed them to go. The first school taught on Denton Creek was in the summer of 1860.

This school was taught in a private house that stood where Dace McDonald's place now stands. Later a double log house was built which served for both school and church. It was built on Cash McDonald's land, two miles southeast of Denver.

The first school taught in the county was in the summer of 1858. The school house stood on the west side of the Perryman graveyard, near Forrestburg.

These schools were subscription schools, as there was no public money to pay salaries. About this time schools began to spring up in different settlements. Names of three of the early teachers were obtained: Sweet, Seely and J. T. Bellows.

The pioneer teacher took his gun with him to school as regularly as he took his lunch, not knowing what moment he would be called upon to protect his pupils and himself from an attack by the savages.

The pioneer settlements were not without the preacher and the missionary, who went about doing good. How many homes these humble men of God have blessed will never be known. Toiling all the week, just as their neighbors did, to obtain the necessaries of life for their families. On Saturday they would saddle their horse, put the well worn Bible in the saddle bags, which was thrown across the saddle and start on a dangerous journey to some distant settlement to preach the word of God. Those days knew no hired preachers. Salaries were unheard of. What pay they received was in provisions of different kinds. No well prepared, well written sermon of thirty minutes would have been tolerated.

On the contrary, the people went expecting to stay several hours, and were rarely disappointed.

In summer the brush arbor was built and the people would come together in good old camp meeting fashion, where they could worship together and sing those religious songs so dear to our mothers: "How Firm a Foundation," "On Jordan's Stormy Banks I Stand," and "There Is a Fountain Filled With Blood."

The following story is told by an early preacher in "Flowers and Fruits of Texas," which abundantly illustrates the truth of the hardships they endured, not only during the days of that period, but all through the pioneer days which followed:

"On a certain trip in the month of March, while passing from one settlement to another, I found a creek swimming, about midway between these two points. About two hours were lost in my efforts to head the swimming water. It was very cold, and I dreaded it. Finally my horse was plunged into the swollen stream. He swam with me to the opposite bank without any difficulty, but as he struggled amid obstructions on the opposite side I was compelled to dismount in the water and give the animal assistance. My boots were full of water, and my clothing thoroughly saturated. A blue Texas norther whistled around my ears and appeared almost to penetrate my quivering limbs, as I mounted the horse at 4 o'clock in the evening, with twenty-five miles lying stretched between me and my destination, and not a single house on the way that I knew of. To my great surprise and gratification, after traveling about eight miles, my clothing now freezing, I came suddenly upon a camp by the roadside, made since my February trip.

"Here was a good fire, a little log cabin, covered, no floor, cracks not lined, and no chimney. A familiar voice was recognized, and a brother whom 1 had known long ago, invited me to share with him for the night the comforts of his camp. He had been there only a short time, had no corn for my horse, and his wagon, sent below for supplies, could not return because of the high waters. It was eighteen miles now to the end of my journey, with two dangerous streams to swim. Although the horse must shiver all night as he nipped the short spring grass, and although the missionary was told the family had neither meat nor bread, he decided to tarry for the night.

"It was by this time almost sunset, and as I drew off my boots and exposed my wet and almost frozen feet to the fire, the good sister gave me a cup of coffee.

"The wind, 'tis true, whistled through the open cracks in the new log cabin, but this was far better than shivering all night alone on the bank of some swollen stream. While drinking my coffee 1 inquired if her husband had guns and ammunition. This was answered in the affirmative.

"I asked if the dogs would tree turkeys. To this

a like answer was returned. Still drinking my coffee I ordered the guns put in good order, assuring the family that my "Master" had a storehouse down in the adjacent creek bottom, and that we would soon have plenty of meat.

"I soon passed out of the cabin with the little boy and the dogs at my heels. The dogs, understanding what was wanted, preceded us into the creek bottom, some half mile distant, and soon the fluttering turkeys were seeking protection in the trees. I was on the ground in double quick, and saw a fine gobbler perched upon a limb almost right over my head. Here I was much perplexed. The turkey stretched his long neck and turned his eye sidewise on me, uttering, 'Put! put!' But the old rifle in my hand had a flint and steel lock, and, holding the gun up in a perpendicular position, I feared when the pan flew open that the powder, instead of taking fire, would empty itself in my eyes. But little time was given to hesitation, and taking aim I shut both eyes and pulled the trigger. Fortunately down came the trigger and no powder entered my eyes. By the time it was dark we went back to camp with several turkeys. One was immediately dressed and hung before the fire in regular backwoods style. This was truly an earnest time for the preacher and the family.

"The clothing I wore was getting a little more comfortable. But on opening my saddle bags I found everything saturated with water from the creek I swam in the afternoon.

"My heart was very sad when I found my old Jerusalem Blade and the old Concordance I had carried twenty-five years perfectly wet. Everything was spread before the fire and the turkey and coffee tasted with a sharp relish. Texans are famous for good, strong coffee, and the flavor of that turkey was beyond description.

"The night's rest was quite refreshing, and as the clear golden sunbeams of the morning appeared, we thanked God together for spiritual and temporal blessings. I bade them good-bye and went on my way without further mishap."

It was nothing unusual for a minister to preach with two six-shooters in his belt, while some stood guard, that the worshipers might not be taken unawares by the Indians.

TEXAS RANGERS.

The Texas rangers were organized in 1859 by the State, and a company was stationed at Brushy Mound, in this county. The commander of this company was Captain John Scanlon. They received pay from the State for their services at this time.

Previous to this they had soldiers stationed at Belknap and other places.

A crisis arose in Montague County when Texas

seceded from the Union. Not only were they called upon to raise companies for the Confederate service, but after the secession the Federal troops were withdrawn and the frontier was left practically unprotected from the Indians. Indian attacks were becoming so frequent that it became necessary for the men to organize what was called "minute men" or "home militia" for the protection of their lives and property.

This organization was a branch of the Confederate service and subject to their regulation. After the war these companies disbanded, and the government put in Northern soldiers. These companies, however, were not large enough to afford a sufficient protection to the people.

After the election of Governor Pease he ordered a regiment of rangers down the frontier to protect the settlers from the Indian attacks. Bud Morris, who was a State ranger on the frontier during the war, was made captain of the first company, and Levi Perryman was appointed captain of the second company. They were given one hundred men each.

Scarcely were they organized, and before they had seen any service, they received orders from General Canby of San Antonio to disband. Immediately following this Bud Morris went to New Orleans to interview General Hancock, commander of the Fifth Military District. He laid before him, in strong terms, a plea for the protection of the helpless frontier against the merciless Indians. But all to no purpose. The general replied to his request very courteously, but told him it was against the policy of the government to allow Southern men to be in arms, that he would furnish ample protection. This he failed to do. Mr. Morris returned and assisted in organizing the home guards and the settlers defended their homes as best they could. After the new Constitution was adopted, when every citizen was allowed to vote, the first officers elected were (so far as could be learned):

W. T. Wayborne, Sheriff and Collector.

Bud Morris, District and County Clerk.

J. A. Gordon, Chief Justice.

According to the Constitution adopted in 1869 each justice of the peace assessed taxes in his own precinct. There was at this time only four precincts in the county. They held what was termed police court, now called "commissioners' court." The Chief Justice (instead of a County Judge, as we now have) presided over this court when the precincts were called together. The Chief Justice performed the regular duties of the justice of the peace, marrying people, issuing writs, etc. All cases that are now tried in our county courts were then tried in the district court. The authority of the Chief Justice extended to about the same authority our justice of the peace now exercises.

Cattle raising was the principal pursuit for many years. As has been stated, the Indians were a great drawback to farming. They would steal the horses, leaving nothing but oxen to plough with, and many times would kill them. Men ploughed wearing two six-shooters in their belts and a Spencer rifle on the plow as protection from the Indians. After the last Indian killing, which is recounted in another chapter, immigration from other States commenced and rapidly increased under the new impulse and encouragement given by the knowledge that the dreaded Indian foe was subdued at last.

In the following chapters we will study something of the progress our county has made from 1858 to 1912, a period of fifty-four years—a little more than half a century.

THE SOUTHLAND.

There the slow river glides down to the sea;
There the wind quivers the vine and the tree;
There the bird voices give life to the air;
All earth rejoices and nature is fair;
There the shy springtime first stops on her way,
Careless what King Time or Winter may say;
There every flower gives home to a bee;
There every hour is happy and free.

Hearts there are truthful, and friendship is dear,
Growing more youthful with love every year.
Honor a boast is, o'er all and before
Kindness stands hostess at each Southern door;

Breezes are blowing o'er valley and hill;
Blossoms are snowing in memory still.
Northland is home, though, and there must I be;
Where'er I roam, though, the Southland for me.
—By S. J. Burnett.

THE UNITED DAUGHTERS OF THE CONFEDERACY.

The boys and girls of our county should become familiar with what the United Daughters of the Confederacy stand for, and why the Southern women engage in the work the organization requires. Such an organization exists in Montague County and has its place in the history of the county, and the records would not be complete without reference to the work of this society.

The United Daughters of the Confederacy had its inception in Nashville, Tenn., where it was the outcome of the women of that city to create a greater interest in preserving the spirit and historic achievements of the South. Its objects have often been stated as being memorial, historical, benevolent, educational and social—to give honor to the memory of those who served and those who fell in the service of the Confederate States.

To record the part taken by the Confederate women in patient endurance and patriotic devotion during the struggle, as well as untiring effort during the reconstruction which followed; to collect and preserve the material for a true history of the war between the States; to preserve historic places of the Confederacy; to fulfill the sacred duties of charity to the survivors of that war and their dependants; to help educate the needy descendants of the worthy Confederates and to cherish the bonds of friendship among the members of the society. With these noble purposes in view they have accomplished much important work. The first organization of this kind in Texas was in 1894. It was not long after this until other Texas cities founded similar organizations, and a State division was formed. Mrs. Kate Cabell Currie of Dallas was chosen as the first president of the division. Under her leadership the chapters received much encouragement.

Their efforts soon broadened, and with the desire to perpetuate the memory of the Southern soldiers, they caused monuments to be erected in their honor in different cities in the State of Texas. The mention of one occasion in particular will serve to show the loyalty of the United Daughters of the Confederacy on many similar occasions.

In the city of Dallas, on May 18, 1896, the ground was broken for the foundation of a great monument to the Confederacy. This monument was to be erected in the City Park. Many of the veterans of this county will remember the invitation sent out to come and pay honor to the Confederate heroes.

The invitation read, "Come on April 28 and 29, 1897, for the monument is completed, and it is a thing of beauty and glory, for not only is the private on his column of gray, but our chieftains are there, too, ready as of old, to stand watch and guard in sunshine and in rain. Yes, come to the love feast we have prepared for you, and to the unveiling ceremonies, for the private is on his pinnacle of glory, and on pedestals at the base are life-size statues of Jefferson Davis, Generals Robert E. Lee, Stonewall Jackson and Albert Sidney Johnston."

From the Capital City of Austin came Governor Culberson to show honor to the Southern soldier. The Legislature closed its doors, and the lawmakers came to show their appreciation of the noble efforts of the United Daughters of the Confederacy (for it was through their untiring effort that the monument was builded), and to do honor to the defenders of their homes. A great multitude had assembled from all parts of the State and from other States. Flags were floating, banners waving, the bands were playing, the bugles calling—the very atmosphere was charged with patriotism. The band took up the strains of "Dixie." This brought forth the old rebel yell, and the people went wild with enthusiasm. It was on this occasion that Mrs. Kate Cabell Currie was presented with a magnificent jeweled badge as a token of appreciation of her faithfulness to the cause.

The United Daughters of the Confederacy of this State have wrought nobly.

The following, according to statistics, are some of the things they have accomplished:

They have carefully examined the histories taught in the schools, correcting errors where possible, calling attention to the bravery of the Confederate soldier, explaining to the young the causes of the war between the States; have secured burial plots for those whose families were unable to provide them and marked the graves with simple marble headstones bearing their names and the company with which they served.

The United Daughters of the Confederacy was organized in Bowie, Montague County, Texas, on the 28th of February, 1900, and has a membership of twenty-seven. The present officers are: Mrs. William A. Ayres, president; first vice president, Mrs. C. C. Hutchison; second vice president, Miss Lydia Benton; secretary, Mrs. Sam Heard; treasurer, Miss Bert Duncan; historian, Mrs. Edgar Edmiston.

This chapter has contributed in many ways to the pleasure and comfort of the Confederate veterans of this county. They have served elegant dinners in their honor, and in 1912 they lighted the Bowie old soldiers' reunion grounds with electricity. They have had a line of wire run from the light plant and placed lights in the pavilion at the barbecue pit and along the amusement trail. The chapter had this work done at their own expense. There may be other chapters in the county, but the above account will serve to show that Montague County is not behind other counties of the State in paying tribute to her soldiers.

November 12, 1912, marked an epoch-making period in the history of the United Daughters of the Confederacy. For the first time in its history the organization met in other than a Southern city. They met in our United States Capital City of Washington for the laying of the corner stone of the new monument to the Confederate soldiers. By act of Congress several years ago a certain section of the Arlington National Cemetery was set apart for the Confederate dead. The monument will stand in the center of this section. When President Taft was Secretary of War he granted to the District of Columbia branch of the United Daughters of the Confederacy permission to erect this Confederate monument. Later the chapters throughout the entire South enlisted in the work. In a metal box placed in the corner stone will rest a copy of the act of Congress authorizing the burial of the Confederate dead in Arlington, a copy of Secretary of War Taft's letter authorizing the raising of the monument, and small silk replicas of the State flags of the various Southern States, and one bearing the Stars and Stripes for the District of Columbia. The War Department co-operated with the U. D. C. in making arrangements.

This brief history of the United Daughters of the Confederacy would not be complete without telling you something of the life of Winnie Davis. Perhaps no woman of the South has been more universally beloved than Winnie Davis, daughter of Jefferson Davis, the first and only President of the Confederacy. She holds a unique place in Southern history. She was the adopted daughter of the South, and was known throughout the length and breadth of the land as "The Daughter of the Confederacy."

One trait of character possessed by this noble woman we would do well to emulate. This trait was loyalty and obedience to her father. Enemies sought to traduce her father's fame, to destroy his life and discredit his patriotism, but she was ever the faithful, sympathetic daughter. To the last she was true to his name, true to the principles for which he struggled and true to the people who loved him.

She was much beloved in Montague County, and her death cast a gloom over the entire South.

A beautiful monument was erected to her memory in Richmond, Va., by contributions from chapters of the United Daughters of the Confederacy all over the South. It contains these inscriptions: On the front, "The beloved child of Jefferson Davis, President of the Confederate States of America, and Varina Howell Davis." On the right side, "Born in the Executive Mansion, Richmond, Virginia, died September 18, 1898, at Narragansett Pier, Rhode Island." On the back, "In the flower of her beauty, rarely gifted in intellect, this noble woman trustfully rendered up her stainless soul to God who gave it. Brave and steadfast, her loyal spirit was worthy of her people's glorious history." On the left side these words appear, "The whole country, touched by her blameless and heroic career, mingled its tears with those who knew and loved her. 'He giveth His beloved sleep.'" At the base of the statue are these words, "In memory of Varina Anne Davis, Daughter of the Confederacy."

In a memorial service held in her honor Colonel Bennett Young of Louisville, Ky., said: "As future generations walk among the reminders of a glorious past there will be no grave amid these renowned and sacred sepulchres which will evoke profounder or gentler emotions, or call forth tenderer memories than that of the adopted child of the Confederacy.

"On the banks of the James River, close to where nearly three hundred years ago came the cavalier, imparting to Southern manhood the uplifting power of his genius, his courage and his chivalry; they have given her lasting sepulchre. The breezes from every hillside, valley and mountain of the Southland shall bear tenderest benedictions to her tomb, and the rippling waters of the stream beside which she rests—fresh from the mountain tops which pierce the blue skies overhanging the mighty Alleghenies—shall murmur softest requiem by her grave, and as these flow into the mighty ocean they will be taken up by the chainless winds which sweep with unbroken power the face of the great deep, and in harmonious melody tell the story to all the world of the marvelous and wondrous love of the people who fought for the lost but glorified cause of the South, for Winnie Davis, the Daughter of the Confederacy."

"THE OLD COAT OF GRAY."

It lies there alone; it is rusted and faded,
    With a patch on the elbow, a hole in the side;
But we think of the brave boy who wore it, and ever
    Look on it with pleasure and touch it with pride.
A history clings to it; over and over
    We see a proud youth hurried on to the fray,
With his frame like the oaks and his eyes like the eagle's,
    How gallant he rode in the ranks of "The Gray."

It is rough, it is worn, it is tattered in places,
    But I love it the more for the story it bears,
A story of courage in struggle with sorrows,
    And a breast that bore bravely its burden of cares.
It is ragged and rusty, but once it was shining
    In the silkiest sheen when he wore it away;

And his face was as bright as the smile of the morning,
  When he sprang to his place in the "Ranks of the Gray."

There's a rip in the sleeve, and the collar is tarnished.
  The buttons all gone with their glitter and gold;
'Tis a thing of the past, and we reverently lay it
  Away with the treasures and relics of old,
As the gifts of love, solemn, sweet and unspoken,
  And cherished as leaves from a long vanished day,
We will keep the old coat for the sake of the loved one
  Who rode in the van in the ranks of "The Gray."

Shot through with a bullet, right here in the shoulder,
  And down there the pocket is splintered and soiled;
Ah! more—see the lining is stained and discolored!
  Yes, blood drops the texture have stiffened and spoiled.
It came when he rode at the head of the column,
  Charging down in the battle one deadliest day,
When squadrons of foemen were broken asunder,
  And victory rode with the ranks of "The Gray."

Its memory is sweetest and sorrow commingled;
  To me it is precious—more precious than gold;
In the rent and the shot hole a volume is written,
  In the stains of the lining is agony told.
That was long years ago, when life's sunny morning,
  He rode with his comrades down into the fray;
And the old coat he wore and the good sword he
    wielded,
  Were all that came back from the ranks of "The
    Gray."

And it lies here alone, I will reverence it ever—
  The patch in the elbow, the hole in the side—
For a gallanter heart never breathed than the loved
    one
  Who wore it with honor and soldierly pride.
Let me brush off the dust from its tatter and tarnish,
  Let me fold it up closely and lay it away,
It is all that remains of the loved and the lost one,
  Who fought for the right in the ranks of "The
    Gray."
                                —"The Veteran."

UNITED CONFEDERATE VETERANS.

The United Confederate Veterans stand for proper loyalty to the Lost Cause and the perpetuation of Southern history. Many a touching story could be told of how the more fortunate veterans have helped their comrades in distress and need. The first United Confederate Veteran camp organized in Montague County was called the "Bob Stone Camp." It was organized about 1880. Bob Bean was chosen captain. The home of this camp is at Nocona. The camp has beautiful grounds here, and each year they have the pleasure of a reunion with their old friends and comrades.

The Bowie Pelham Camp, No. 572, United Confederate Veterans, was organized in 1895. The membership increased, reaching a total enrollment of one hundred and two. In 1901 the camp bought twenty-seven and one-half acres of land east of town for a park. In 1905 a pavilion was built in the park, and since that time improvements have been added from time to time. Three wells of splendid water have been drilled and the water supply is abundantly sufficient for all purposes. A large barbecue pit built of stone, a mess house and a long dining shed with tables for one hundred plates are a part of the conveniences. The park is all fenced and ample hitching and camping grounds are provided for those coming from a distance. The camp has the park and all improvements entirely paid out, and derives an annual revenue of $50 from a small portion of the ground, leased for agricultural purposes. The veterans take great pride in their park, and well they may, for it is one of the finest in Northwest Texas. Beautiful groves are dotted here and there. Roads leading from town to the park have made it easily accessible.

Bowie Pelham Camp has an annual reunion. Once in its history it has had the honor of entertaining the State reunion, and once they entertained the veterans of the Quantrell and Shelby commands. The present officers of the camp for 1912 are: J. A. Cummins, captain; J. M. Stallings, first lieutenant; J. F. Donald, second lieutenant; S. H. Lancaster, chaplain; G. W. Herron, adjutant; J. W. Slaughter, historian; F. G. Hankins, color sergeant.

It is most interesting to listen to the veterans as, in reminiscent mood, they exchange stories of "before the war," "during the war" and "after the war;" and to see how their eyes sparkle and their steps quicken to the sound of Dixie.

Perhaps you do not know who wrote the song called Dixie—for Dixie's land and the South are synonymous terms the world over. "Dixie" was composed by Daniel Decatur Emmett of Mount Vernon, Ohio. In his early days he was an actor, and when he became old and infirm the "Actor's Fund" of New York contributed five dollars a week toward his support. The contributions came regularly for a long time, when, for some unexplained cause, they were discontinued. He made an appeal for help to the South and a generous amount was sent him. The Southern people were touched to learn of the poverty of this man, whose parents were Southern born, and to know that the writer of "Dixie," the most inspiring air known to Southern people, was in distress. The following history of the song is given by a friend of the composer:

"This dear old song, which has given its author, Daniel Decatur Emmett, imperishable fame, has become so thoroughly identified with one section of our country that it may be doubted whether or not it is entitled to be classed among our national songs; although it is the opinion of a great many that it should be so classed—but it is confidently asserted that had it not been for the divisions created by the great civil strife it would have been as popular in the North today as in the South, since it first came out in the North and achieved almost instant popularity there, the boys taking it up on the streets. It must be generally conceded, whether it is sectional or not, that there are but few songs which have more power to move a popular audience in any geographical section of our country than has this soul-stirring melody. Dixie was taken up and adopted by the South. This is as Mr. Emmett intended it should be; he meant by 'Dixie' the land of the South, according to his own testimony. Dixie was written in the spring of 1859 and always carried with it the idea of the South, which he clearly indicated by the words, 'The land of cotton,' and other like expressions."

Mr. Emmett also wrote another song, which became exceedingly popular throughout the country. The name of this song was "Old Dan Tucker," and was quickly taken up by the children, but "Dixie," which has power to raise a Southern audience to its feet anywhere, and to cause a stir of enthusiasm among any people, is perhaps the most lively and inspiring air that the musical world has ever known. But the old Confederate veterans who once marched to the air of this thrilling melody, will soon be gone. The morning for them is over, and the long shadows of evening are gathering about the followers of Robert E. Lee, Stonewall Jackson and Albert Sidney Johnston.

Be kind and respectful to them, ever remembering that they have given us a splendid history of a splendid people who fought for a splendid principle. Be as loyal to your country as they were to their "cause," and you will make noble citizens.

PROGRESSIVE MONTAGUE COUNTY.

There is an imaginary plain in the minds of men called "the plains of time."

If the children of Montague County were permitted to visit the highest point of this plain and look back from that lofty view over the ground that has been traversed by the pioneers of this county, what would they behold by way of contrast between the past and present?

First would come the Indian, the original inhabitant, with his war paint and feathers, sweeping over the prairies, accompanied by hundreds of warriors in pursuit of game. They would see rolling prairies, hills and wooded spots, with groups of mustang ponies grazing here and there.

And what is that queer looking animal just over yonder with a hump on its back?

That is the buffalo. They one time roamed the prairies in large herds, but the constant inroads made upon them by early hunters who came here from time to time almost exterminated them.

At present there is a herd on the "Good Night ranch" in West Texas, and a few in Brackenridge Park, in San Antonio. With these exceptions we know of no others left of the vast herds that once existed. The events following the advent of the first white people who came to Montague County to found their homes, the critical periods through which they passed, constitute the beginning of the real history of Montague County.

What you should seek to store up in your memories are the efforts toward successful progress made by these pioneers.

A remarkable development has been brought about by the rapidity with which the population of the county has increased.

From a comparatively unsettled district in 1857, it has grown to the present population of 24,800 souls.

Our natural resources have had much to do with this, but they would not avail without enterprise and intellect.

Events have followed each other in rapid succession. "Indian Depredations," "War and Reconstruction Days," all retarded the growth of the county.

Agriculture was not followed extensively until after 1874.

Yet, in spite of many drawbacks, the county has steadily progressed until by contrast the student can see, whereas in 1874 only a few bales of cotton were raised in Montague County, there were grown in 1909-10, 21,705 bales.

Amount of cotton produced in the county, 1910-11, 28,435 bales.

While the raising of cattle, hogs, horses, mules, sheep and goats is not the principal pursuit, statistics show there are 27,172 cattle, 13,576 horses and mules, 12,714 hogs and 636 sheep and goats in the county.

Cotton raising is the principal industry, but Montague County early learned that her soil was adapted to many growths.

The coming of the railroad in 1882 gave immediate facilities for transportation and the people were not slow to take advantage of it.

After this period fruit farming was engaged in extensively, and where can there be found peaches, apples or pears grown to greater perfection than in the orchards of Montague County.

Apples from the Davis apple orchard at Fruitland, this county, took first prize at the St. Louis World's Fair.

Thousands of bushels of fruit of different varieties are shipped to other markets from Montague County, while an abundance remains for home consumption.

The people are coming to believe more and more in diversified farming, and large crops of berries, potatoes, peanuts and grapes are grown each year.

Market gardening is being developed on a larger scale, splendid crops of tomatoes and other vegetables being grown for market.

Corn, oats, wheat and alfalfa are also grown successfully.

Intensive methods of farming are being observed, and some wonderful crops have been raised by scientific methods, and some surprising results have been obtained from unresponsive soil by following the advice of government farm experts.

The "Boys' Corn Clubs" are creating a great deal of interest along this line.

This has been the greatest century in civil and political progress, as well as inventions to be applied to industrial life.

In no field of effort have inventors been more ac

tive or their results been more successful than in the invention of labor saving devices.

Montague County has shared in the use of these inventions and who among us can fail to appreciate the worth this has been to agriculture?

Compare the progress from the old time sickle and scythe, the old-fashioned plow and spade, and the hand gathered harvest to the present modern implements that have so marvelously increased the working power of the farmer.

Probably no American inventions have been more widely used than the new agricultural machines, cultivators, planters, seeders, reapers, mowers, harvesters, corn huskers and shellers and numerous other labor saving inventions which have added thousands of dollars to the farmers' bank account.

In marked contrast to the rude log cabins of the early settlers are the cosy, comfortable, beautiful homes now to be seen in every part of the county.

Civic attractiveness is getting a great hold on the people, and it is the ambition of nearly every home owner to beautify his grounds.

Children are being taught the value and beauty of trees and flowers. Many of the smaller children have their little plots of ground for their very own, where they can cultivate flowers and vegetables.

In early days a "road working" was unknown, from the simple fact that they had no roads, nor were there any bridges across the creeks.

Imagine starting across the country with a heavily laden wagon drawn by slow moving oxen, blazing out your own road and crossing the creeks as best you could, and you will have some idea of the means of transportation in the fifties.

Today Montague County is greatly interested in the road question. A special road tax of 15 cents on the hundred dollars is used to improve the public highways of the county, and it is not uncommon to see the citizens wearing a button that announces to the world that, "I favor pike roads." All of this has tended to enhance the value of land.

In the early days some of the best land in the county sold as low as $3 per acre. Now, improved land ranges in price from $15 to $50 per acre.

Unimproved land is quoted at $8 to $12 per acre.

Water is obtained at an average depth of fifty feet.

The rainfall approximates thirty-two inches per annum.

The upland farming section is composed mostly of a sandy loam. This soil holds the moisture well, consequently it does not require as much rain to produce a crop as other soils. The elevation of the county varies. At Montague, the county seat, it is 1075 feet. Along the streams is to be found a black sandy loam with stretches of deep clay. Wild grape vines, dogwood, walnut, pecan, cottonwood and elm trees flourish, while in the springtime the trees are filled with songsters, the ground is carpeted with violets, and the woods are redolent with the odor of wild plum blossoms.

A red clay is found in the valleys.

The surface is undulating and about equally divided between prairie and timber. Traces of oil have been found and many farms in the county have been leased to oil companies for the purpose of developing this industry. The trees of this section, with a few exceptions on the bottom lands, do not grow to a very great size. Other trees peculiar to this county are the postoak, liveoak and black jack.

While the timber was not very large it furnished the only material at hand for constructing the first homes of the county, some of which are still standing as a record of the thrift and industry of those days.

Formerly the trees were made into rails with which the fences around large tracts of land were built.

The rail fence has been relegated to the background, and in its place is the barbed wire fence. When this mode of fencing came into use it greatly reduced the labor of the farmers, for it took a long time to make enough rails to fence a farm. Now they only have to make the fence posts, to which the wire is fastened by means of staples.

The county made wonderful strides in prosperity in these years.

Crops were abundant and the area under cultivation was rapidly increasing. The wealth of the county had greatly increased and public business had become so large that it became necessary to found a bank.

The first bank in the county was founded in 1884 at Montague.

Since then there have been quite a number of banks instituted in the county, which are generally an evidence that a county is prospering.

The first newspaper published in the county was in 1874. The editor was Willie Lyles. Before the civil war his father was one of the wealthiest lawyers in Memphis, Tennessee. He was also a colonel in the Confederate army. When the war was over he found his father's wealth all gone and Willie came to Texas to engage in the newspaper business.

He went to Montague and there established the "Montague News." A newspaper in those days was a precious article, and was carefully preserved, to be referred to on many occasions.

Now the county has a number of well established weekly newspapers in different towns of the county.

These papers exchange items of interest from the respective towns, and in this way the people are kept in touch with local affairs all over the county, while a large number of our modern citizens would as soon miss a meal as to do without their daily papers.

One of the first stores in the county was established at Montague in 1858. This store was owned by Cox & Davis. They hauled their goods from Shreveport and Jefferson, Louisiana. With our modern facilities we can travel more quickly from New York to San Francisco than the pioneer merchant could transport his merchandise from Louisiana to Texas.

Now the county has well managed, well established dry goods, grocery, hardware, furniture and drug stores.

The people do not have to go away from home for any of the necessities and but few of the luxuries of life.

Few buggies or carriages were seen in the early eighties. Now there is scarcely a farmer who does not possess either a hack, buggy or carriage for family use.

Briefly summed up, from a thinly settled district in the fifties, our county, through a period of successive developments, has reached a high standard of civilization.

The county has three railroads, the Fort Worth & Denver, the Chicago & Rock Island and the M., K. & T.

The church property of the county amounts to many thousands of dollars, most of the various denominations being represented.

This is an age of fraternal organization, and there is considerable property throughout the country owned by the different lodges.

Cotton gins, flour mills and oil mills furnish employment for a large number of men.

There are also two creameries in the county, one at Bowie, the other at Nocona. The people who live along the route traversed by the North Texas Gas Company have the privilege of burning gas for light and fuel. In pioneer days our mothers read their Bibles by the light of a home-made tallow candle, sitting before a fire of logs. Their daughters read the latest novel beneath a gas or an electric light and sit before a grate that is heated by gas, wood or coal.

Had an automobile crossed the prairie at night in the early fifties, with its two shining eyes of immense proportions, and its resounding honk, honk, it could have put to flight a thousand superstitious Indian warriors, and no doubt would have created a mild excitement among the sturdy settlers.

The automobile is so common in Montague County now they have long since failed to create the interest they did in former days.

The county supports two public institutions, the jail for the detention of prisoners and the county farm for the care of the indigent.

A number of the towns of the county have organized what is known as commercial clubs. These clubs are composed of public spirited citizens whose purpose is to advertise the county and to encourage activity along all lines looking to the development of the county. One of the means by which the advancement of a city or county may be determined is by the postoffice receipts, county valuations and school enrollment.

The property valuation of Montague County is twelve million dollars. Scholastic population of the county, 6233.

Bowie is the largest town in the county. The postoffice receipts at this place for the past five years, 1907-1912, are as follows:

1907..........$8,414.35   1908..........$8,779.91
1909.......... 9,425.92   1910.......... 9,933.84
1911.......... 9,175.22

Money orders issued (Domestic).		International
1907	$5,603	16
1908	6,094	12
1909	7,321	22
1910	7,479	27
1911	7,268	21
Money orders paid (Domestic):		International
1907	$2,730	none.
1908	2,347	none.
1909	2,763	none.
1910	2,357	none.
1911	2,689	one.

Number of postoffices in the county, 15; number of rural routes in the county, 27.

Bowie has six rural routes.

Poll tax paid for 1911 total 3834.

EXECUTIVE DEPARTMENT OF MONTAGUE COUNTY.

What is government?

Ans. Government is defined as rule or control.

Why is government necessary?

Ans. That the stronger may not encroach upon the weaker, that justice may be meted out, that property and personal rights may receive protection and that peace and order may prevail. Good government is necessary to useful action.

Under what form of government do the people of Montague County live?

Ans. A republican form of government.

What is a republican form of government?

Ans. It is a government under which the people rule themselves through representatives of their own selection.

What is a county?

Ans. A circuit or particular portion of a State or kingdom separated from the rest of the territory.

Why were counties organized?

Ans. For the purpose of bringing justice nearer the people and to establish a medium for the transactions to be carried on with the State.

How is a county organized?

Ans. By act of the Legislature.

Do all counties possess the same area?

Ans. They do not, but vary greatly in size in different portions of the State.
When was Montague County created?
Ans. In 1857.
When organized?
Ans. In 1858.
For whom was the county named?
Ans. For Colonel Daniel Montague.
What is the area of Montague County?
Ans. Nine hundred and seventy-six square miles.
In what Senatorial District is Montague County?
Ans. Thirty-first Senatorial District.
What counties does this district embrace?
Ans. Montague, Denton and Wise counties.
Name the different officers of the county.
Ans.
1. Representative.
2. County Judge.
3. County Clerk.
4. County Attorney.
5. County Treasurer.
6. Superintendent Public Schools.
7. Tax Assessor.
8. District Clerk.
9. Tax Collector.
10. Sheriff.
11. County Commissioners.

How many Commissioners does the county require?
Ans. Three.

How many Justices of the Peace does this county require?

Ans. Eight.

How many voting precincts in the county?

Ans. Twenty-three.

What is the duty of the Representative?

Ans. To endeavor to bring about the enactment of laws that will be for the interest and welfare of the people.

What is the duty of the County Judge?

Ans. He has jurisdiction of wills and estates, appoints administrators and guardians, holds examining trials and appoints officers of election.

What is the duty of the County Attorney?

He is the county's legal adviser and represents the county in all civil suits to which it may be a party. It is his duty to prosecute the accused in trials of crimes in the county court and in the justice's court.

Define the duties of a County Clerk.

The Clerk is the recording officer of the county court, issues writs, preserves papers and enters judgments on record and issues marriage license.

What is the duty of the County Treasurer?

Ans. He is the chief financial officer of the county, and keeps a record of the receipts and expenditures of the county. He is required to give bond for the faithful performance of his duties.

What is the duty of the Tax Assessor?

Ans. To get a rendition of the property of each citizen and the valuation of same.

What is the duty of the District Clerk?

To compile the docket and look after all matters pertaining to the work of the district court.

What is the duty of the Tax Collector?

Ans. To collect the taxes that have been assessed against the property of the county.

What is the duty of the Superintendent of Public Schools?

Ans. It is his duty to look after the affairs, as concerns the welfare of our public schools. He examines teachers, issues teachers' certificates, holds teachers' institutes, visits the schools, advises the teachers in regard to their duties, and reports the condition of school interests to the State Superintendent.

What are the duties of the Sheriff?

Ans. The Sheriff is guardian of the peace in the county, and its chief executive officer. He arrests persons charged with crime, serves writs and has charge of the county jail and prisoners.

What are the duties of County Commissioners?

Ans. They have charge of the county property, such as the court house, jail, poor farm, etc., and erect county buildings, construct county bridges, improve the public highways and represent the county as a financial board.

What are the duties of a Justice of the Peace?

Ans. To preside over the justice courts, write

deeds, perform marriage ceremonies and to assess fines for offenses committed within his jurisdiction.

Name the present county officers.

Name the Senator for this district.

Who are the legal voters of Montague County?

Ans. All male citizens, twenty-one years of age, and in possession of a poll tax receipt, are recognized as qualified voters in this county.

What is the duty of a citizen?

To respect and obey the law, to labor for the public welfare, to assist in securing justice, to submit to the will of the majority, to vote for such candidates and measures that, according to his judgment, will contribute most to the public welfare; to insist that all children attend the public schools.

Upon the walls of the Congressional Library at Washington are engraved these words, which are fraught with so much significance: "The foundation of every State is the education of its youth." Texas early recognized the truth of these words. In 1839, during the administration of President Lamar, an effort was made to establish a system of public schools. President Lamar, himself a scholar and a statesman, in his message to the Third Congress of Texas, in 1839, said:

"The cultivated mind is the guardian genius of democracy, and while guided and controlled by virtue, is the noblest attribute of man. It is the only dictator that free men acknowledge, and the only security that free men desire.''

In 1839 each county was granted three leagues of land for school purposes, and in 1840 another league was added, while fifty leagues were set apart for a State University.

I would not have you think that during all of these pioneer years you have been reading about that the people of Montague County were unmindful of the importance of education. They only awaited an opportunity to assist in the advancement of public schools. And, as will be seen, the citizens are thoroughly alive to the importance of public education. In 1839 Montague County was a wild, unsettled region, peopled only by the Indians, and it was not until thirty-nine years later that there was any effort made toward the development of schools. In 1878 the first public school was taught in the county. The teachers made the best progress possible with their limited facilities. From a few poorly equipped schools, with small attendance, scattered here and there in 1880, the county now has one hundred and eight schools with a property valuation of thousands of dollars, employing an average of two hundred teachers in the county. The county has been divided into school districts. These are composed of two classes: the independent school district and the common school district. The common school district is created by the Commissioners' Court. The independent school districts are incorporated by vote of the people for school purposes and created by special act of the Legislature, and cities and towns that have assumed control of their schools.

There are 114 counties in Texas which have a County Superintendent of Public Schools. Of this number Montague County is one. The County Superintendent has direct supervision of the common school districts and independent districts of less than 150 population and receive their school fund from the county treasury. The Legislature recently enacted a law that will be of far-reaching benefit not only to the school districts of Montague County, but to the entire State. This was the enactment of the rural high school law. This law provides for a county board of education in each county, and their duty shall be to classify the schools of the county into high schools, intermediate schools and primary schools. And it will also be their duty to suggest a course of study in co-operation with the County Superintendent, subject to the rules and regulations of the State Department of Education. At a meeting held in this county at Montague in 1912 the County Board of Trustees classified the schools of the county. The schools were classified under the late school laws of the State as follows: In addition to the Ringgold, Spanish Fort and Mallard, Forrestburg and Stoneburg schools, which had previously been classed as high schools, Dye Mound, New Harp, Oak Bluff.

Pleasant Ridge and Leona schools, were put into the high school class, and all other schools of the county were classed as intermediate schools, with the privilege of teaching high school subjects, provided they employ two teachers, one of whom must hold a first grade certificate. The independent school districts of the county are not under the control of the County Board of Trustees. The County Board for 1912 is composed of Dr. W. W. Crain of Nocona, chairman; W. S. Taylor, Queen's Peak; W. F. Landers, Forrestburg; W. G. Bralley, Montague; O. P. Hill, Eureka. County Superintendent W. W. Snodgrass is secretary of the County Board.

This extension of our school system ought to stimulate the desire of the pupils to enjoy these larger opportunities. Education is one of the most important subjects that can claim the attention of the boys and girls of Montague County. National history abundantly illustrates the truth that the power and poise of the person of education cannot be estimated. But let us remember, pupils, that education is not to make us appear greater to the world, but that the world may appear greater to us, and that this thought may help us to take a broader view of life, and enable us to impart beauty and richness and grace to other lives. This is the duty we owe the world. Education only fits us to better carry out that duty. Speaking of teachers, their desire to have their pupils advance, etc., our county teachers have the privilege of attending one of three State Normals—the Sam Houston Normal, located at Huntsville; the North Texas Normal, located at Denton, and the West Texas Normal, located at Canyon City. The third grade certificate which once existed in our county has been abolished, and each year makes it harder for the teacher holding a second grade certificate to obtain a school. All teachers, before they are qualified to teach in the high school grades, must possess a first grade certificate.

The scholastic population of Montague County in 1911 was 6,156; in 1910, 6,233. There is every evidence of progress in the school life of the county in the numerous, modern, well equipped school buildings in various parts of the county. Montague County's apportionment of State school fund in 1911-12 was $41,860.80. Twenty years ago local school tax was unknown in Montague County, now the school tax approximates $50,000 per year. This money is paid by the people for the maintenance of public schools. The local school tax was first voted in this county in 1886. Liberty Chapel was the first school in Montague County to take this step. The average school term has increased from seventy-five days to one hundred days, showing an increase of twenty-five days over the old terms. Montague County boasts of a splendid business college. This school is located in Bowie and is known as the Bowie Commercial College. They have an actual business system that is invaluable to the pupil. The youngest bank president in the South is a graduate of this college. A distinctly modern innovation in the public schools is the organization of the Mother's Club. This organization co-operates with the teachers and pupils, striving to bring their interests closer together, and enleavoring to cultivate a spirit of civic pride, and, by the assistance of the teachers, create within the child a love for the beautiful in surroundings. This county has a number of towns, Bowie being the largest town in the county, having a population of five thousand. Other towns of the county are Sunset, Fruitland, Denver, Ringgold, Stoneburg, Belcher, Nocona, Bonita, Mallard, Forrestburg, Dye Mound, Uz, New Harp, Hardy, Gladys, Spanish Fort and Montague. Montague is the county seat. Montague County is bordered on the north by Red River, but has no rivers flowing through the county. There are a number of streams in the county—Sandy, Brushy, Elm, Denton, Clear Creek, Mountain Creek, Belknap, Salt Creek and Farmers' Creek.

When we review the history of Montague County from its organization in 1858 on through the various changes down to 1912 we ask ourselves the question, Why should we be always looking back into the past ages for examples of heroism? Why not study some lessons of patriotism at home? These lessons are taught in the lives of our own fathers. Such is the history of Montague County.

Years have passed since the first settlements were made. Now it is filled with beautiful farms, and teeming with towns, railroads, schools and churches.

Discord and contention, though bitter while they lasted, have borne only the peaceful fruit of harmony, and one of the greatest of the Texas counties has entered upon a splendid career and the ample foundation of a prosperous and successful citizenship has been securely laid.

PATRIOTISM.

This book will have lost its purpose if it fails to instill within our growing citizens a feeling of patriotism for their county, their State and their country. When it is said that patriotism is an important question, it is said in the fullest expression of the term. It is important because it involves principles of home and national pride.

Patriotism is a rich heritage, and it is upon this inheritance that the security of our nation is resting. On it depends a happy people.

Unpatriotic people are restless, dissatisfied, hard to please. Look, for example, at the mass of foreign element constantly pouring into our country. They come to our glorious shores for freedom, glad to leave their mother country, to breathe the patriotic air of America, where they train desirable citizens for worthy missions. The time has come when the faith of the boys and girls must be strengthened by thoughts of constancy. This virtue is taught in the annals of the early settlers of this county, and in the lives of the first defenders of this country. We should never lose an opportunity to show our appreciation and respect for what they have done for us.

Loyalty to one's country is a beautiful sentiment, and the question arises as to how many of our boys and girls know "My Country, 'Tis of Thee," "Columbia" and "The Star Spangled Banner," and how many of them rise when our national hymn is played in their hearing?

Is it not time that the American people direct the thoughts of our future citizens along this line of education in order to encourage that feeling of "pride of country" so essential to our public welfare?

A group of foreigners were standing on a crowded thoroughfare in one of our American cities when the band struck up "America." One of the group remarked that the American people displayed so little enthusiasm over their national music. In foreign countries the people have to pay every respect to their national airs to please their rulers, but in freedom-loving America it should please the American people to accord honor to their country on every occasion, for it is the greatest of all the great countries of the world.

It is hoped the time will come when every boy and girl in Montague County will sing "America," "Hail Columbia" and the "Star Spangled Banner" with the "spirit and the understanding." It will interest the boys and girls to know something of the origin of these songs, a brief history of which is as follows:

The author of that grand, soul-thrilling song, "America," was Dr. Samuel Francis Smith of Newton Center, Mass. Not long ago a movement was started to preserve the old home of the author, and to make it a place where souvenirs connected with the poet and song writer may be gathered together, to be viewed by both the present and future generations. Dr. Smith was nature's poet, as may be imagined by his songs and poems. As he contemplated the beauty and grandeur of his own, his native land, his patriotic soul burst forth in song and he gives to the world these glorious verses:

"My country, 'tis of thee, sweet land of Liberty,
    Of thee I sing: Land where my fathers died,
    Land of the Pilgrim's pride, from every mountain side
Let freedom ring.

"My native country, thee, land of the noble free,
    Thy name I love; I love thy rocks and rills,
    Thy woods and templed hills, my heart with rapture thrills,
Like that above.

"Let music swell the breeze, and ring from all the
        trees,
    Sweet freedom's song; let mortal tongues awake,
    Let all that breathes partake, let rocks their si-
        lence break,
The sound prolong.

"Our father's God to thee, author of liberty,
    To thee we sing; long may our land be bright
    With freedom's holy light! Protect us by thy
        might,
Great God, our King.

This hymn was first sung in public at a children's Fourth of July celebration in 1832, in the old Park Street Church, Boston.

"Hail Columbia" was written by Joseph Hopkinson in 1798. The writer claims for this song the distinction of having brought about peaceable relations between France and America, when war seemed inevitable. The poet tells in the following words how he came to write "Hail Columbia:"

The contest between England was raging and the people of the United States were divided into parties for the one side or the other. The object of the author was to create an American sentiment which should, independent of and above the interests, passions and policies of both belligerents, cause them to look and feel exclusively for our honor and rights. The song found instant favor with both parties, to which the author, whether wisely or not, attributes the most gratifying results. The words are:

"Hail Columbia, happy land, hail ye heroes,
    Heaven-born band,
Who fought and bled in freedom's cause,
Who fought and bled in freedom's cause,
And when the storm of war was gone,
Enjoyed the peace your valor won;
Let independence be our boast,
Ever mindful what it cost,
Ever grateful for the prize,
Let its altar reach the skies.

    Chorus—
"Firm, united let us be, rallying round our liberty,
As a band of brothers joined,
Peace and safety shall we find.

"Immortal patriots, rise once more,
Defend your rights, defend your shore
Let no rude foe, with impious hand,
Let no rude foe, with impious hand,
Invade the shrine where sacred lies,
Of toil and blood, the well earned prize,
While offering peace sincere and just;
In heaven we place a manly trust,
That truth and justice shall prevail,
And every scene of bondage fail."

"The Star Spangled Banner, another of our national airs, was written by Francis Scott Key in 1814, under the most trying circumstances. The writer was being held a prisoner on board a British vessel while the British were bombarding Fort McHenry. As he paced the deck in doubt as to what would be the outcome, he drew out an envelope and scribbled the outline of the "Star Spangled Banner." It has been often said of this song that it breathes the purest patriotism. While "America" is called the national hymn of the republic, the "Star Spangled Banner" is called our "National Hymn." The words of this inspiring song are:

"Oh, say, can you see, by the dawn's early light,
  What so proudly we hailed at twilight's last gleaming,
Whose broad stripes and bright stars through the perilous fight,
  O'er the ramparts we watched were so gallantly streaming?
And the rocket's red glare, the bombs bursting in air,
  Gave proof through the night that our flag was still there.

  Chorus—
"Oh, say, does that Star Spangled Banner yet wave,
O'er the land of the free and the home of the brave?
On the shore dimly seen, through the mists of the deep,

Where the foe's haughty host in dread silence re-
poses,
What is that which the breeze, o'er the towering
steep,
As it fitfully blows, half conceals, half discloses?
Now it catches the gleam of the morning's first beam,
In full glory reflected, now shines on the stream:
'Tis the star spangled banner, oh, long may it wave
O'er the land of the free and the home of the brave.

"And where is that band who so vauntingly swore
That the havoc of war and the battle's confusion,
A home and a country should leave us no more?
Their blood has washed out their foul footsteps'
pollution.
No refuge could save the hireling and slave,
From the terror of flight or the gloom of the grave.
And the 'Star Spangled Banner' in triumph doth
wave
O'er the land of the free and the home of the brave.

"Oh, thus be it ever, when free men shall stand
Between their loved home, and wild war's desola-
tion;
Blest with vict'ry and peace, may the heaven's res-
cued land
Praise the Power that hath made and preserved
us a nation.

Then conquer we must, when our cause it is just, and this be our motto,
In God is our trust! And the Star Spangled Banner in triumph shall wave
O'er the land of the free and the home of the brave."

CPSIA information can be obtained at www.ICGtesting.com
Printed in the USA
LVOW02s1318301113

363313LV00007B/413/P